O9-BTM-205

1st EDITION

Perspectives on Diseases and Disorders

Meningitis

Sylvia Engdahl
Book Editor

PERSPECTIVES
On Diseases & Disorders

GALE
CENGAGE Learning™

Detroit • New York • San Francisco • New Haven, Conn • Waterville, Maine • London

Christine Nasso, *Publisher*
Elizabeth Des Chenes, *Managing Editor*

© 2010 Greenhaven Press, a part of Gale, Cengage Learning

For more information, contact:
Greenhaven Press
27500 Drake Rd.
Farmington Hills, MI 48331-3535
Or you can visit our Internet site at gale.cengage.com

For product information and technology assistance, contact us at

Gale Customer Support, 1-800-877-4253
For permission to use material from this text or product, submit all requests online at www.cengage.com/permissions

Further permissions questions can be e-mailed to permissionrequest@cengage.com

Articles in Greenhaven Press anthologies are often edited for length to meet page requirements. In addition, original titles of these works are changed to clearly present the main thesis and to explicitly indicate the author's opinion. Every effort is made to ensure that Greenhaven Press accurately reflects the original intent of the authors. Every effort has been made to trace the owners of copyrighted material.

Cover image © Jeff Morgan health/Alamy

LIBRARY OF CONGRESS CATALOGING-IN-PUBLICATION DATA

Meningitis / Sylvia Engdahl, book editor.
   p. cm. -- (Perspectives on diseases and disorders)
 Includes bibliographical references and index.
 ISBN 978-0-7377-4790-4 (hardcover)
 1. Meningitis--Popular works. I. Engdahl, Sylvia.
 RC124.M525 2010
 616.8'2--dc22

                                                    2009052340

Printed in the United States of America
1 2 3 4 5 6 7 14 13 12 11 10

Date: 07/30/12

616.82 MEN
Meningitis /

CONTENTS

Rosalyn Carson-DeWitt

Meningitis, or inflammation of the membranous
covering of the brain and spinal cord, is usually
caused by bacteria, viruses, or fungi. Bacterial
meningitis is not common but can progress very
rapidly and can be fatal.

Christian Nordqvist

There are many different types of meningitis. Fast
treatment is needed, so it is important to know
what symptoms to look for.

Amanda Gardner

Rates of pneumococcal meningitis have declined
substantially in all age groups since Prevnar,
a vaccine for infants and young children, was
introduced.

CHAPTER 2 Issues Concerning Meningitis

security. Moreover, requiring students in college housing to get it is a violation of their rights.

CHAPTER 3 Personal Narratives About Meningitis

FOREWORD

"Medicine, to produce health, has to examine disease."
—Plutarch

Independent research on a health issue is often the first step to complement discussions with a physician. But locating accurate, well-organized, understandable medical information can be a challenge. A simple Internet search on terms such as "cancer" or "diabetes," for example, returns an intimidating number of results. Sifting through the results can be daunting, particularly when some of the information is inconsistent or even contradictory. The Greenhaven Press series Perspectives on Diseases and Disorders offers a solution to the often overwhelming nature of researching diseases and disorders.

From the clinical to the personal, titles in the Perspectives on Diseases and Disorders series provide students and other researchers with authoritative, accessible information in unique anthologies that include basic information about the disease or disorder, controversial aspects of diagnosis and treatment, and first-person accounts of those impacted by the disease. The result is a well-rounded combination of primary and secondary sources that, together, provide the reader with a better understanding of the disease or disorder.

Each volume in Perspectives on Diseases and Disorders explores a particular disease or disorder in detail. Material for each volume is carefully selected from a wide range of sources, including encyclopedias, journals, newspapers, nonfiction books, speeches, government documents, pamphlets, organization newsletters, and position papers. Articles in the first chapter provide an authoritative, up-to-date overview that covers symptoms, causes and effects, treatments, cures, and medical advances. The second chapter presents a substantial number of opposing viewpoints on controversial treatments and other current debates relating to the volume topic. The third chapter offers a variety of personal perspectives on the disease or disorder. Patients, doctors, caregivers, and loved ones represent just some of the voices found in this narrative chapter.

Each Perspectives on Diseases and Disorders volume also includes:

- An **annotated table of contents** that provides a brief summary of each article in the volume.
- An **introduction** specific to the volume topic.
- Full-color **charts and graphs** to illustrate key points, concepts, and theories.
- Full-color **photos** that show aspects of the disease or disorder and enhance textual material.
- **"Fast Facts"** that highlight pertinent additional statistics and surprising points.
- A **glossary** providing users with definitions of important terms.
- A **chronology** of important dates relating to the disease or disorder.
- An annotated list of **organizations to contact** for students and other readers seeking additional information.
- A **bibliography** of additional books and periodicals for further research.
- A detailed **subject index** that allows readers to quickly find the information they need.

Whether a student researching a disorder, a patient recently diagnosed with a disease, or an individual who simply wants to learn more about a particular disease or disorder, a reader who turns to Perspectives on Diseases and Disorders will find a wealth of information in each volume that offers not only basic information, but also vigorous debate from multiple perspectives.

INTRODUCTION

Imagine what it would be like to wake up in a hospital and find that you no longer had feet or even legs. That is what has happened to some people, many of them children or teenagers, after they came down with bacterial meningitis—a disease that until recently few people had even heard of. It is not a new disease, but it is rare in most parts of the world. Until recently it was not a disease the public worried about. Now, in part because a new vaccine has become available, more attention is being called to it.

The term *meningitis* refers to inflammation of the membranes that cover the brain and spinal cord. Bacterial meningitis, also called meningococcal disease, is the most damaging form. Many of its victims die, often within a day or two of developing symptoms. It is especially serious when it progresses to meningococcal septicemia, or blood poisoning, which, even when not fatal, can lead to gangrene and the amputation of limbs. New drugs have been developed to treat the disease, and as a result more patients survive than in the past. But that very success has created new problems.

"We've become so much better at resuscitating kids, there's so much more we can do for them than ever before," said Joseph Britto, a consultant at St. Mary's Hospital in London, England, to a reporter for the British newspaper the *Observer*. "But, although those kids might come through, what we can't do is bring them through intact. It's such a devastating disease there are often severe after-effects."[1]

Linda Glennie, head of research at Britain's Meningitis Research Foundation, said: "By rescuing children who would otherwise die, we have far more kids alive with amputations. Even kids who don't end up with brain damage often end up with some softer intellectual damage—such as problems with memory, co-ordination, or learning abilities."[2]

Because the disease is uncommon, stories about individual young people stricken by it are newsworthy and often appear in local papers. There are also many personal stories at the Web sites of organizations that fight meningitis. Many of these are about teens who have overcome the damaging effects of meningitis and gone on to be successful in school or in sports despite having artificial limbs. Others are written by the grieving parents of those who died suddenly, some of whom have created Web sites of their own to urge other parents to get their children vaccinated.

Recently, since the development of a vaccine, Menactra, that is effective against four of the five types of meningococcal disease, the Centers for Disease Control and Prevention (CDC) has recommended vaccination for everyone between the ages of eleven and eighteen. Though the disease can strike young children and adults, too, their risk of contracting it is lower. Close contact with groups is the principal risk factor, and therefore residents of college dormitories and military barracks are especially vulnerable. At many colleges it is now mandatory for students who live in dorms either to receive a vaccination or sign a waiver, and as of 2009 this requirement is the law in about half the states. Vaccination is also recommended for international travelers of all ages.

Statistically, getting meningococcal disease is unlikely in the United States; it occurs in only about three thousand people each year. For this reason some officials believe that it is not cost-effective to devote public health resources to its prevention. But because its effects are so serious, more and more experts have come to feel that people should be made aware of the danger. Cases are not always recognized soon enough even by doctors, for meningitis is easily mistaken for the flu. Yet the consequences of delay are severe. Antibiotics can treat it effectively, but only if it is diagnosed at an early stage. The first symptoms are high fever, headache, and stiff neck; later there may be vomiting, sensitivity to light, confusion, and a red or purple rash. These symptoms can progress very quickly, and if they do, death can occur within hours. For those who do not die, there are often permanent effects—such as brain damage, damage to organs, hearing loss, or learning disabilities—whether or not septicemia develops.

There are other forms of meningitis besides meningococcal disease, but they are of lesser concern. HiB meningitis, the type of bacterial meningitis that used

In India a doctor gives an injection to a child stricken with bacterial meningitis. **(Prakash Singh/AFP/ Getty Images)**

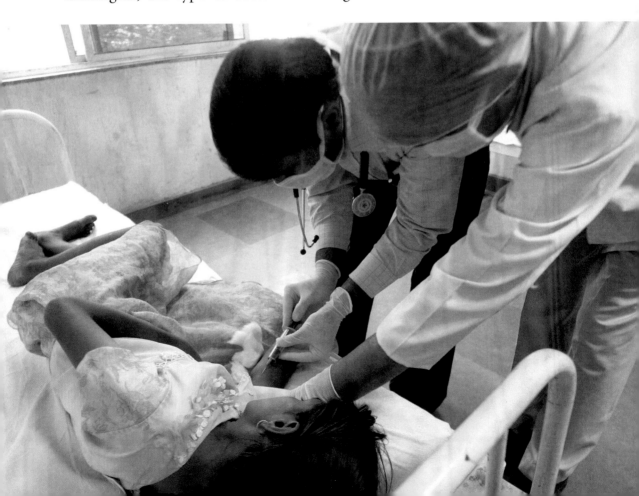

to be the most prevalent, has been nearly wiped out in North America and many other countries because a vaccine against it is routinely given to babies. Pneumococcal meningitis, which affects mainly young children, has now also been greatly reduced by routine vaccination. Viral meningitis—caused by a virus rather than by bacteria—is common, but it is less severe than bacterial meningitis and usually requires no treatment. Beside these, there are a number of uncommon causes against which no precautions need be taken except by people with weakened immune systems.

Meningococcal disease is much more prevalent in Africa than in the rest of the world. Because there is a shortage of vaccines in Africa and those available do not provide long-term protection, it has been the practice in most African countries to undertake mass vaccination only in areas where there are outbreaks. In a section of sub-Saharan Africa known as the meningitis belt, which has an at-risk population of about 430 million, epidemics often occur. The worst one was in 1996, when there were more than 250,000 cases and 25,000 reported deaths. Another exceptionally serious breakout occurred in early 2009. Many medical teams from the international humanitarian organization Doctors Without Borders, working alongside local health authorities, treated sick patients and vaccinated more than 7 million people. A new vaccine against meningitis A, MenAfriVac—which is more effective and less expensive than the older ones used in African countries—was introduced in 2009. There are plans to immunize a population of approximately 250 million one- to twenty-nine-year-olds and 23 million infants by 2015. However, insufficient supplies were available to help with the 2009 epidemic.

In the United States there is plenty of vaccine available, and although it does not provide complete protection since one of the five types of meningococcal disease is not prevented by it, it does protect against the most common ones. Why then are there so many young people who do not receive it? Some refuse for religious, philosophical, or medical reasons, and some cannot afford it; but the main reason, at least among college students, is simply lack of information. That was the case with Derek Horn, a Pennsylvania teen who spent four days in a medically induced coma to combat bacterial meningitis that had first appeared to be the flu. Horn did not need amputations, but he nearly died, and later, during his long rehabilitation, he could not stand up without a walker. Vaccination had not been required of him by his college because he lived at home rather than in a dorm. "I didn't even really know what it was or anything," he told a reporter. "They asked me at the doctor's office, 'Do you want it?' and I said no."[3]

Notes

1. Quoted in Anthony Browne, "Medicine's Tragic Price," *Observer*, November 4, 2001. www.guardian .co.uk/education/2001/nov/04/medicalscience.health.
2. Quoted in Browne, "Medicine's Tragic Price."
3. Quoted in Dan Berrett, "Scary Lesson for Pennsylvania Teen Who Declined Vaccine," *Fort Wayne Journal Gazette*, July 12, 2009. www.journalgazette.net/article/ 20090712/LOCAL04/907129981/0/FRONTPAGE.

CHAPTER 1

Understanding Meningitis

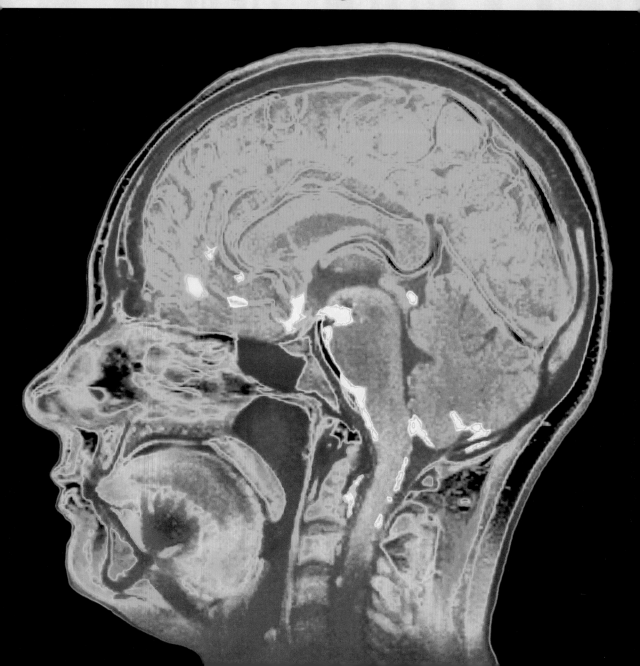

An Overview of Meningitis

Rosalyn Carson-DeWitt

In the following selection Rosalyn Carson-DeWitt explains what meningitis is and how it affects the brain. She then discusses different types of meningitis, what causes them, and how they are diagnosed, followed by an explanation of treatment, prognosis, and prevention. Carson-DeWitt is a medical editor, writer, and consultant. She has edited several medical encyclopedias and has written thousands of articles for health-care providers and consumers.

Meningitis is a serious inflammation of the meninges, the thin, membranous covering of the brain and the spinal cord. Meningitis is most commonly caused by infection (by bacteria, viruses, or fungi), although it can also be caused by bleeding into the meninges, cancer, diseases of the immune system, and an inflammatory response to certain types of chemotherapy or other chemical agents. The most serious

SOURCE: Rosalyn Carson-DeWitt, *Gale Encyclopedia of Medicine.* Belmont, CA: Gale, 2006. Copyright © 2006 by Thomson Gale. Reproduced by permission of Gale, a part of Cengage Learning.

Photo on facing page. In this colored magnetic resonance imaging scan of a woman's brain, meningitis appears in yellow. (**Simon Fraser/ Photo Researchers, Inc.**)

and difficult-to-treat types of meningitis tend to be those caused by bacteria. In some cases, meningitis can be a potentially fatal condition.

The Brain

Meningitis is a particularly dangerous infection because of the very delicate nature of the brain. Brain cells are some of the only cells in the body that, once killed, will not regenerate themselves. Therefore, if enough brain tissue is damaged by an infection, serious, life-long handicaps will remain.

In order to learn about meningitis, it is important to have a basic understanding of the anatomy of the brain. The meninges are three separate membranes, layered together, which encase the brain and spinal cord:

- The dura is the toughest, outermost layer, and is closely attached to the inside of the skull.
- The middle layer, the arachnoid, is important because of its involvement in the normal flow of the cerebrospinal fluid (CSF), a lubricating and nutritive fluid that bathes both the brain and the spinal cord.
- The innermost layer, the pia, helps direct blood vessels into the brain.
- The space between the arachnoid and the pia contains CSF, which helps insulate the brain from trauma. Many blood vessels course through this space.

CSF, produced within specialized chambers deep inside the brain, flows over the surface of the brain and spinal cord. This fluid serves to cushion these relatively delicate structures, as well as supplying important nutrients for brain cells. CSF is reabsorbed by blood vessels located within the meninges. A careful balance between CSF production and reabsorption is important to avoid the accumulation of too much CSF.

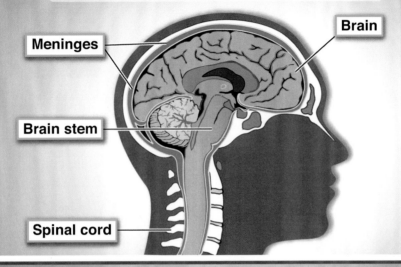

Meningitis and the Brain

In meningitis the meninges that line the brain become swollen and inflamed.

Meninges

Brain

Brain stem

Spinal cord

Taken from: Human Illness and Behavioral Health, www.humanillness.com.

Because the brain is enclosed in the hard, bony case of the skull, any disease that produces swelling will be damaging to the brain. The skull cannot expand at all, so when the swollen brain tissue pushes up against the skull's hard bone, the brain tissue becomes damaged and may ultimately die. Furthermore, swelling on the right side of the brain will not only cause pressure and damage to that side of the brain, but by taking up precious space within the tight confines of the skull, the left side of the brain will also be pushed up against the hard surface of the skull, causing damage to the left side of the brain as well.

Another way that infections injure the brain involves the way in which the chemical environment of the brain changes in response to the presence of an infection. The cells of the brain require a very well-regulated environment. Careful balance of oxygen, carbon dioxide, sugar (glucose), sodium, calcium, potassium, and other substances must be maintained in order to avoid damage to brain tissue. An infection upsets this balance, and brain damage can occur when the cells of the brain are either deprived of important nutrients or exposed to toxic levels of particular substances.

The cells lining the brain's tiny blood vessels (capillaries) are specifically designed to prevent many substances from passing into brain tissue. This is commonly referred to as the blood-brain barrier. The blood-brain barrier prevents various substances that could be poisonous to brain tissue (toxins), as well as many agents of infection, from crossing from the blood stream into the brain tissue. While this barrier is obviously an important protective feature for the brain, it also serves to complicate treatment in the case of an infection by making it difficult for medications to pass out of the blood and into the brain tissue where the infection is located.

Causes of Meningitis

The most common infectious causes of meningitis vary according to an individual's age, habits, living environment, and health status. While nonbacterial types of meningitis are more common, bacterial meningitis is the more potentially life-threatening. Three bacterial agents are responsible for about 80% of all bacterial meningitis cases. These bacteria are *Haemophilus influenzae* type b, *Neisseria meningitidis* (causing meningococcal meningitis), and *Streptococcus pneumoniae* (causing pneumococcal meningitis).

In newborns, the most common agents of meningitis are those that are contracted from the newborn's mother, including Group B streptococci (becoming an increasingly common infecting organism in the newborn period), *Escherichia coli*, and *Listeria monocytogenes*. The highest incidence of meningitis occurs in babies under a month old, with an increased risk of meningitis continuing through about two years of age.

Older children are more frequently infected by the bacteria *Haemophilus influenzae, Neisseria meningitidis*, and *Streptococci pneumoniae*.

Adults are most commonly infected by either *S. pneumoniae* or *N. meningitidis*, with pneumococcal meningitis the more common. Certain conditions predispose to this type of meningitis, including alcoholism and chronic upper respiratory tract infections (especially of the middle ear, sinuses, and mastoids).

N. meningitidis is the only organism that can cause epidemics of meningitis. In particular, these have occurred when a child in a crowded day-care situation or a military recruit in a crowded training camp has fallen ill with meningococcal meningitis.

Viral causes of meningitis include the herpes simplex virus, the mumps and measles viruses (against which most children are protected due to mass immunization programs), the virus that causes chicken pox, the rabies virus, and a number of viruses that are acquired through the bites of infected mosquitoes.

FAST FACT

In early 2009, after years of research, scientists discovered how the deadly meningococcal bacteria is able to break through the body's natural defense mechanism and attack the brain.

A number of medical conditions predispose individuals to meningitis caused by specific organisms. Patients with AIDS (acquired immune deficiency syndrome) are more prone to getting meningitis from fungi, as well as from the agent that causes tuberculosis. Patients who have had their spleens removed, or whose spleens are no longer functional (as in the case of patients with sickle cell disease) are more susceptible to other infections, including meningococcal and pneumococcal meningitis.

The majority of meningitis infections are acquired by blood-borne spread. A person may have another type of infection (of the lungs, throat, or tissues of the heart) caused by an organism that can also cause meningitis. If this initial infection is not properly treated, the organism will continue to multiply, find its way into the blood stream, and be delivered in sufficient quantities to invade past the blood-brain barrier. Direct spread occurs when an organism spreads to the meninges from infected tissue next to or very near the meninges. This can occur, for example, with a severe, poorly treated ear or sinus infection.

Patients who suffer from skull fractures possess abnormal openings to the sinuses, nasal passages, and middle ears. Organisms that usually live in the human respiratory system without causing disease can pass through openings caused by such fractures, reach the meninges, and cause infection. Similarly, patients who undergo surgical procedures or who have had foreign bodies surgically placed within their skulls (such as tubes to drain abnormal amounts of accumulated CSF) have an increased risk of meningitis.

Organisms can also reach the meninges via an uncommon but interesting method called intraneural spread. This involves an organism invading the body at a considerable distance away from the head, spreading along a nerve, and using that nerve as a kind of ladder into the skull, where the organism can multiply and cause meningitis. Herpes simplex virus is known to use this type of spread, as is the rabies virus.

Symptoms of Meningitis

The most classic symptoms of meningitis (particularly of bacterial meningitis) include fever, headache, vomiting, sensitivity to light (photophobia), irritability, severe fatigue (lethargy), stiff neck, and a reddish purple rash on the skin. Untreated, the disease progresses with seizures, confusion, and eventually coma.

A very young infant may not show the classic signs of meningitis. Early in infancy, a baby's immune system is

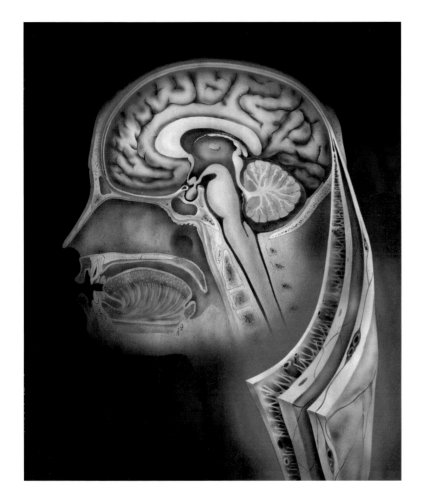

This illustration highlights the meninges, the outer covering of the brain and central nervous system. Meningitis attacks the three layers of the meninges and causes inflammation and edema. (**Jim Dowdalls/ Photo Researchers, Inc.**)

not yet developed enough to mount a fever in response to infection, so fever may be absent. Some infants with meningitis have seizures as their only identifiable symptom. Similarly, debilitated elderly patients may not have fever or other identifiable symptoms of meningitis.

Damage due to meningitis occurs from a variety of phenomena. The action of infectious agents on the brain tissue is one direct cause of damage. Other types of damage may be due to the mechanical effects of swelling and compression of brain tissue against the bony surface of the skull. Swelling of the meninges may interfere with the normal absorption of CSF by blood vessels, causing accumulation of CSF and damage from the resulting pressure on the brain. Interference with the brain's carefully regulated chemical environment may cause damaging amounts of normally present substances (carbon dioxide, potassium) to accumulate. Inflammation may cause the blood-brain barrier to become less effective at preventing the passage of toxic substances into brain tissue.

Diagnosis of Meningitis

A number of techniques are used when examining a patient suspected of having meningitis to verify the diagnosis. Certain manipulations of the head (lowering the head, chin towards chest, for example) are difficult to perform and painful for a patient with meningitis.

The most important test used to diagnose meningitis is the lumbar puncture (commonly called a spinal tap). Lumbar puncture (LP) involves the insertion of a thin needle into a space between the vertebrae in the lower back and the withdrawal of a small amount of CSF. The CSF is then examined under a microscope to look for bacteria or fungi. Normal CSF contains set percentages of glucose and protein. These percentages will vary with bacterial, viral, or other causes of meningitis. For example, bacterial meningitis causes a greatly lower than normal percentage of glucose to be present in CSF, as the bacteria are essentially "eating" the host's glucose, and using it for their own nutrition and energy production. Normal CSF should contain no infection-fighting cells (white blood cells), so the presence of white blood cells in CSF is another indication of meningitis. Some of the withdrawn CSF is also put into special lab dishes to allow growth of the infecting organism, which can then be identified more easily. Special immunologic and serologic tests may also be used to help identify the infectious agent.

In rare instances, CSF from a lumbar puncture cannot be examined because the amount of swelling within the skull is so great that the pressure within the skull (intracranial pressure) is extremely high. This pressure is always measured immediately upon insertion of the LP needle. If it is found to be very high, no fluid is withdrawn because doing so could cause herniation [rupture] of the brain stem. Herniation of the brain stem occurs when the part of the brain connecting to the spinal cord is thrust through the opening at the base of the skull into the spinal canal. Such herniation will cause compression of those structures within the brain stem that control the most vital functions of the body (breathing, heart beat, consciousness). Death or permanent debilitation follows herniation of the brain stem.

Treatment of Meningitis

Antibiotic medications (forms of penicillin and cephalosporins, for example) are the most important element of treatment against bacterial agents of meningitis. Because of the effectiveness of the blood-brain barrier in preventing the passage of substances into the brain, medications must be delivered directly into the patient's veins (intravenously, or by IV), at very high doses. Antiviral drugs (acyclovir) may be helpful in shortening the course of viral meningitis, and antifungal medications are available as well.

Other treatments for meningitis involve decreasing inflammation (with steroid preparations) and paying careful attention to the balance of fluids, glucose, sodium, potassium, oxygen, and carbon dioxide in the patient's system. Patients who develop seizures will require medications to halt the seizures and prevent their return.

Prognosis and Prevention

Viral meningitis is the least severe type of meningitis, and patients usually recover with no long-term effects from the infection. Bacterial infections, however, are much more severe, and progress rapidly. Without very rapid treatment with the appropriate antibiotic, the infection can swiftly lead to coma and death in less than a day's time. While death rates from meningitis vary depending on the specific infecting organism, the overall death rate is just under 20%.

The most frequent long-term effects of meningitis include deafness and blindness, which may be caused by the compression of specific nerves and brain areas responsible for the senses of hearing and sight. Some patients develop permanent seizure disorders, requiring life-long treatment with anti-seizure medications. Scarring of the meninges may result in obstruction of the normal flow of CSF, causing abnormal accumulation of CSF. This may be a chronic problem for some patients, requiring the installation of shunt tubes to drain the accumulation regularly.

Prevention of meningitis primarily involves the appropriate treatment of other infections an individual may acquire, particularly those that have a track record of seeding to the meninges (such as ear and sinus infections). Preventive treatment with antibiotics is sometimes recommended for the close contacts of an individual who is ill with meningococcal or *H. influenzae* type b meningitis. A meningococcal vaccine exists, and is sometimes recommended to individuals who are traveling to very high risk areas. [The vaccine is now recommended for all persons eleven to eighteen years of age.] A vaccine for *H. influenzae* type b is now given to babies as part of the standard array of childhood immunizations.

The Causes and Symptoms of Meningitis

Christian Nordqvist

In the following article Christian Nordqvist explains what causes different kinds of meningitis and lists the symptoms that are important for people to look for. He describes a simple test that can be implemented at home to determine whether or not a rash is caused by meningitis. Information about the treatment of meningitis is also included. Nordqvist is the editor of Medical News Today.

The word "meningitis" comes from the Modern Latin word *meninga* and the Greek word *Menix* meaning "membrane". The suffix "itis" comes from the Greek word *itis* meaning "pertaining to". In medical English, the suffix "-itis" means "inflammation of". The membranes that surround the brain and the spinal cord are collectively known as the *meninges—meningitis* means inflammation of the *meninges*. According to Medilexicon's medical dictionary, meningitis is *"Inflammation of the membranes of the brain or spinal cord"*. . . .

SOURCE: Christian Nordqvist, "What Is Meningitis? What Causes Meningitis?" Medical News Today, May 19, 2009. www.medicalnews today.com. Reproduced by permission.

What Causes Meningitis?

Meningitis is generally caused by infection of viruses, bacteria, fungi, parasites, and certain organisms. Anatomical defects or weak immune systems may be linked to recurrent bacterial meningitis. In the majority of cases the cause is a virus. However, some non-infectious causes of meningitis also exist.

Bacteria mimic human cells to get in and stay in. A study carried out by researchers at the University of Oxford and Imperial College London, England, revealed the way in which bacteria that cause bacterial meningitis mimic human cells is to evade the body's innate immune system.

- Viral meningitis. Although viral meningitis is the most common, it is rarely a serious infection. It can be caused by a number of different viruses, such as mosquito-borne viruses. There is no specific treatment for this type of meningitis. In the vast majority of cases the illness resolves itself within a week without any complications.
- Bacterial meningitis. Bacterial meningitis is generally a serious infection. It is caused by three types of bacteria: *Haemophilus influenzae* type b [HiB], *Neisseria meningitidis,* and *Streptococcus pneumoniae* bacteria. Meningitis caused by *Neisseria meningitidis* is known as meningococcal meningitis, while meningitis caused by *Streptococcus pneumoniae* is known as pneumococcal meningitis. People become infected when they are in close contact with the discharges from the nose or throat of a person who is infected.

  Twenty years ago [HiB] was the main cause of bacterial meningitis—it is not any more thanks to new vaccines which are routinely administered to children.

  The doctor needs to know what type of meningitis has infected the patient. Certain antibiotics can stop some types from infecting others.

This illustration depicts invading *Neisseria meningitidis* bacteria attacking the meningeal layer of the brain. (**Jim Dowdalls/Photo Researchers, Inc.**)

- Bacterial meningitis in newborns and premature babies. A type of *streptococci*, called group B *streptococci* commonly inhabits the vagina and is a common cause of meningitis among premature babies and newborns during the first week of life. *Escherichia coli*, which inhabit the digestive tract, may also cause meningitis among newborns. Meningitis that occurs during epidemics can affect newborns—*Listeria monocytogenes* being the most common.
- Bacterial meningitis in children under 5. Children under five years of age in countries that do not offer the vaccine are generally infected by *Haemophilus influenzae* type B.

- Bacterial meningitis in older children. Older children generally have meningitis caused by *Neisseria meningitidis* (meningococcus), and *Streptococcus pneumoniae* (serotypes 6, 9, 14, 18 and 23).
- Bacterial meningitis in adults. About 80% of all adult meningitis are caused by *N. meningitidis* and *S. pneumoniae*. People over 50 years of age have an increased risk of meningitis caused by *L. monocytogenes*.
- Bacterial meningitis and people with skull damage implanted devices. People who received a recent trauma to the skull are at increased risk of bacteria in their nasal cavity entering the meningeal space. Patients with a cerebral shunt or related device also run a higher risk of infection with *staphylococci* and *pseudomonas* through those devices.
- Bacterial meningitis and weak immune systems. People with weak immune systems are also at higher risk of infection with *staphylococci* and *pseudomonas*.
- Bacterial meningitis and ear infections and procedures. Rarely, otitis media, mastoiditis, or some infection to the head or neck area may lead to meningitis. People who have received a cochlear implant run a higher risk of developing pneumococcal meningitis. . . . Another study found that children who are stricken with severe hearing loss are five times more likely to contract meningitis.

    In countries where tuberculous meningitis is common, there is a higher incidence of meningitis caused by *Mycobacterium tuberculosis*.
- Anatomical defects or disorders of the immune system. Either congenital or acquired anatomical defects may be linked to recurrent bacterial meningitis. An anatomical defect might allow a way to penetrate into the nervous system from the external

environment. The most common anatomical defect which leads to meningitis is skull fracture, especially when the fracture occurs at the base of the brain, or extends towards the sinuses and petrous pyramids.

59% of recurrent meningitis cases are due to anatomical defects, while 36% are due to weakened immune systems.

What Are the Symptoms of Meningitis?

As meningitis and septicemia tend to show similar symptoms and incidences of both tend to rise and fall at the same time in geographical areas, this section refers to both meningitis and septicemia.

Meningitis is not always easy to recognize. In many cases meningitis may be progressing with no symptoms at all. In its early stages, symptoms might be similar to those of flu. However, people with meningitis and septicemia [a blood infection] can become seriously ill within hours, so it is important to know the signs and symptoms. Early symptoms of meningitis broadly include:

- Vomiting
- Nausea
- Muscle pain
- High temperature (fever)
- Headache
- Cold hands and feet
- A rash that does not fade under pressure. This rash might start as a few small spots in any part of the body—it may spread rapidly and look like fresh bruises. This happens because blood has leaked into tissue under the skin. The rash or spots may initially fade, and then come back.

FAST FACT

According to the National Meningitis Association, meningococcal disease strikes nearly three-thousand Americans each year, and 10 to 12 percent of those affected die. Among the survivors approximately 20 percent live with permanent disabilities such as brain damage, hearing loss, or loss of limbs.

The Symptoms of Meningitis

Not everyone gets all these symptoms, and they can appear in any order.

Meningococcal Septicemia		Meningitis	
Rash	●		
Log pain	●		
Cold hands and feet	●		
Floppy child/ difficulty supporting own weight	●	●	
Fever, vomiting, or diarrhea	●	●	
Confusion and drowsiness	●	●	
Difficulty breathing	●		
Abdominal/joint/ muscle pain	●		
Abnormal skin color	●		
Severe headache		●	
Stiff neck		●	
Dislike of bright light		●	
Body stiffens/jerky movements		●	

Taken from: Meningitis UK, "Meningitis? Know the Symptoms," www.meningitisUK.org.

In babies, you should look out for at least one of the following symptoms:

- a high-pitched, moaning cry
- a bulging fontenelle
- being difficult to wake
- floppy and listless or stiff with jerky movements
- refusing feeds
- rapid/unusual/difficult breathing
- pale or blotchy skin
- red or purple spots that do not fade under pressure

In older children, you should look out for:

- a stiff neck
- severe pains and aches in your back and joints
- sleepiness or confusion
- a very bad headache (alone, not a reason to seek medical help)
- a dislike of bright lights
- very cold hands and feet
- shivering
- rapid breathing
- red or purple spots that do not fade under pressure

What Is the Glass Test?

- Press the side of a drinking glass firmly against the rash.
- If the rash fades and loses color under pressure it is not a meningitis rash.
- If it does not change color you should contact a doctor immediately.

What Is the Treatment for Meningitis?

In an interesting study, UK [United Kingdom] researchers looked at whether children with suspected meningitis should be given antibiotics before their transfer to hospital. Meningitis treatment will generally depend on four main factors:

- The age of the patient
- The severity of the infection
- What organism is causing it?
- Are other medical conditions present?

Viral meningitis will resolve itself fairly quickly and does not usually need any medical treatment. If symptoms continue after two weeks the person should see his/her doctor.

The treatment for severe meningitis, which is nearly always bacterial (but can be viral), may require hospitalization, and includes:

- Antibiotics—usually administered intravenously by injection, or through an IV.
- Corticosteroids—if the patient's meningitis is causing pressure in the brain, corticosteroids, such as dexamethasone, may be administered to adults and children.
- Acetaminophen (paracetamol)—effective in bringing the patient's temperature down. Other methods for reducing the patient's fever may include a cool sponge bath, cooling pads, plenty of fluids, and good room ventilation.
- Anti-convulsants—if the patient has seizures (fits), he/she will be given an anti-convulsant, such as phenobarbital or dilantin.
- Oxygen therapy—if the patient has breathing difficulties oxygen therapy may be given. This may involve a face mask, a nasal cannula, a hood, or a tent. In more severe cases a tube may be inserted into the trachea via the mouth.
- Fluid control—dehydration is common for patients with meningitis. If a meningitis patient is dehydrated he/she may develop serious problems. It is

crucial that he/she is receiving adequate amounts of fluids. If the patient is vomiting, or cannot drink, liquids may be given through an IV.

• Blood tests—measuring the patient's blood sugar and sodium is important, as well as other vital body chemicals.

• Sedatives—these are given if the patient is irritable or restless.

If the meningitis is severe the patient may be placed in an ICU (intensive care unit).

Scientists at the University of Nottingham have finally discovered how the deadly meningococcal bacteria is able to break through the body's natural defence mechanism and attack the brain. This could lead to better treatment and vaccines for meningitis.

The Success of Infant Vaccination Against Pneumococcal Meningitis

Amanda Gardner

In the following article Amanda Gardner reports that there has been a large decline in rates of one of the types of meningitis, pneumococcal meningitis, since the vaccine Prevnar became standard for children under two years old. There has been a significant effect not only on the children themselves but on adults, which suggests a "herd immunity" effect—that is, the more people in a community who are immune to a disease, the less likely even an unvaccinated person will be exposed to it. Gardner is a reporter for HealthDay.

Rates of pneumococcal meningitis, a potentially life-threatening infection, have declined substantially since a new vaccine was introduced in 2000, a new study shows.

The declines have been seen not only in children given the vaccine but also in adults, suggesting a herd immunity effect, the researchers noted. To assess the effect of the vaccine, researchers from several universities analyzed surveillance data from 1998 to 2005 in eight states.

SOURCE: Amanda Gardner, "Meningitis Vaccine Seems to Work Like a Charm," HealthDay, January 14, 2009. www.healthday.com. Reproduced by permission.

Overall, the number of cases of the disease dropped 30 percent in that time, but the effect on the very youngest and oldest was even more pronounced: Incidence decreased by 64 percent in those younger than 2 and by 54 percent in those older than 65.

Types of Meningitis

Viral meningitis	Also known as aseptic meningitis. Common, especially among young children, but less serious than bacterial meningitis.
HiB meningitis	Formerly the most common form of bacterial meningitis; has been nearly eradicated in North America by routine infant vaccination.
Pneumococcal meningitis	Formerly common in infants and young children; incidence has declined significantly because of vaccination.
Meningococcal disease A	The most common form in Africa; vaccination recommended for travelers.
Meningococcal disease B	The most lethal form. No vaccine available as of 2009.
Meningococcal disease C	The most common form in North America.
Meningococcal disease W135	Rare in North America but has become common in Saudi Arabia; vaccination required of people making pilgrimages to Mecca.
Meningococcal disease Y	Has recently become more common in North America.
Fungal meningitis	Also known as cryptococcal meningitis. Affects mainly people with compromised immune systems such as those with AIDS.
Other	A number of rare forms exist.

[Compiled by editor.]

"This vaccine has really had a very profound effect on the incidence of pneumococcal disease," said study co-author Dr. Nancy Bennett, a professor of medicine at the University of Rochester Medical Center, in New York. The report appears in the Jan. 15 [2009] issue of the *New England Journal of Medicine*.

The study goes beyond previous research in terms of looking at population groups as well as different forms of *Streptococcus pneumoniae*, which causes pneumococcal meningitis, an inflammation of the meninges, or membranes, surrounding the brain and spinal cord.

"This is a pretty comprehensive study looking at a number of different serotypes [groupings of bacteria within a family] and all age groups. It gets a nice survey of the population," said Jeffrey Cirillo, an associate professor of microbial and molecular pathogenesis at Texas A&M Health Science Center College of Medicine, in College Station. "It is only in eight states so it's not throughout the entire country, but it's probably the most comprehensive analysis, and no one else had looked at it over that long of a period."

Standard Vaccine for Infants

The vaccine, known as Prevnar and made by Wyeth Pharmaceuticals, is part of the standard vaccination recommendation for children in the United States ages 2 to 23 months, as well as for children 24 to 59 months old who are at high risk for pneumococcal disease.

Since the vaccine came out in 2000, there have been a number of studies reporting on its effect on meningitis and blood infections.

"This is the first to focus specifically on meningitis," Bennett said.

There was a 73.3 percent decrease in the incidence of PCV7 serotype (bacteria types covered by the vaccine) in all age groups. Researchers also found declines in antibiotic-resistant serotypes not specifically targeted by the vaccine.

"There were small increases in the rates of meningitis caused by serotypes that are not included in the vaccine," Bennett noted. The study reported a 60.5 percent increase in cases of meningitis types not protected by the vaccine, but Bennett said that "even a 60 percent increase in something that doesn't happen much has a small effect overall."

The increases were "outweighed by the overall decrease in disease," she said.

However, she continued, "it is something that we need to closely observe and that will be addressed with vaccines that cover more serotypes."

Prevnar was developed by researchers at the University of Rochester, who sold the technology to Wyeth,

A recently developed vaccine, Prevnar (spelled "Prevenar" in some countries), has shown to be effective in treating pneumococcal meningitis in children under two years old. **(Dr. P. Marazzi/Photo Researchers, Inc.)**

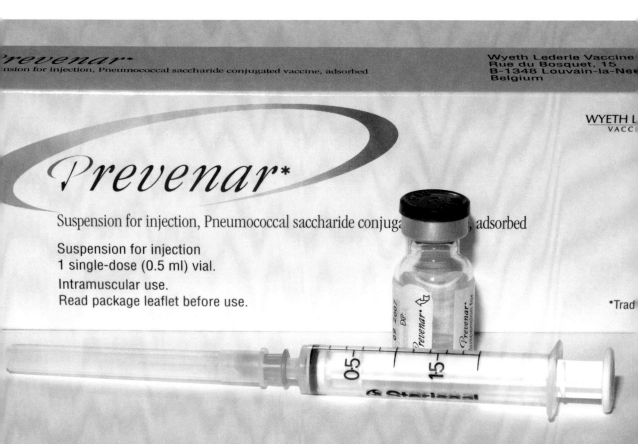

according to a university spokesman. Several authors of the study, including Bennett, have received funding from Wyeth and other pharmaceutical companies.

Cirillo described the study results as "very promising."

"This is a pretty significant finding, especially the large impacts the vaccine has on serotypes it covers," he said. "And within the serotypes that were covered, the efficacy was up to about 90 percent," referring to certain groups that showed the incidence of pneumococcal meningitis decreasing by almost 93 percent. "That's amazing."

A Major Meningitis Epidemic in Africa

Doctors Without Borders

The following report from Doctors Without Borders (known as MSF, the initials of its French name, Médecins Sans Frontières) tells of the organization's success in vaccinating people in western Africa during the meningitis epidemic of 2009. Early in that year more than sixty-five thousand people were infected and at least two thousand died. MSF, in cooperation with national health officials, vaccinated more than 7.3 million people, and as a result the death toll was relatively low. MSF is an international medical humanitarian organization that provides aid in nearly sixty countries to people whose survival is threatened by violence, neglect, or catastrophe.

T he huge emergency response to a meningitis outbreak in West Africa, mainly in Nigeria and Niger, is almost over now [May 2009]. During the last four months, Doctors Without Borders/Médecins Sans Frontières (MSF) teams in cooperation with national health officials have been moving quickly, following the

SOURCE: Doctors Without Borders, "West Africa: Major Meningitis Epidemic Nears End," May 15, 2009. Reproduced by permission.

epidemic trend, to help treat tens of thousands of patients and to move swiftly in a vaccination campaign for 7.5 million people.

The magnitude and length of meningitis outbreak in West Africa required a huge effort in response, beginning early in the season, in January, and just about to end. Since the start of the year, more than 65,000 people have been infected in the areas where MSF launched emergency operations; northern Nigeria, southern Niger and in the south of N'Djamena, capital of Chad.

The epidemic was one of the largest in a region known for years as the "meningitis belt". At least 2,132 people have died. In total, around 7.5 million people were immunized during the outbreak by joint teams made up of national health ministries and MSF.

Emergency Mobilization

With MSF support, health ministries monitored the epidemic's evolution across hundreds of thousands of square kilometers containing about 44 million people, more than the total population of Spain. The large-scale mobilization included 200 international staff (mainly doctors, nurses, and logisticians), 7,500 local staff, and Ministry of Health staff.

"In a typical day, our teams cover the 34 local government areas in Katsina State," explains Dr Laurentia Enesi, of Katsina State, Nigeria. "We have to provide health staff with adequate drugs and equipment or training when needed. People infected with meningitis might die or develop complications if they are not treated quickly enough."

Up to 400 vaccination teams of five people each immunized thousands of people every day in the region for a few weeks. In total, 2.8 million people were vaccinated

> **FAST FACT**
>
> Meningitis epidemics regularly hit African countries in the area referred to as the "meningitis belt," which stretches across the continent from Senegal to Ethiopia. The total population at risk in these countries is about 300 million.

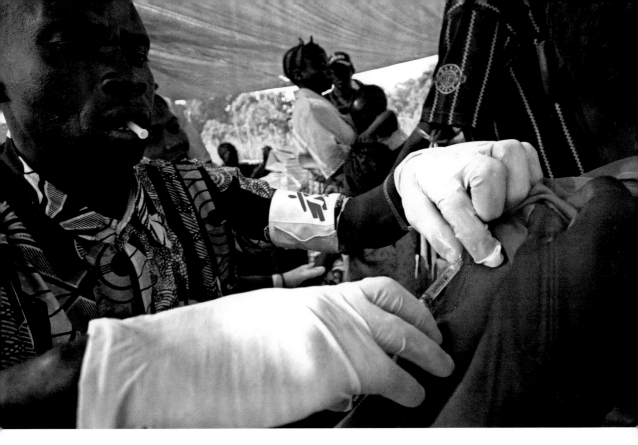

in Zinder, Maradi, and Dosso regions in Niger, and 4.5 million people in Katsina, Jigawa, Bauchi, Kebbi, Sokoto, Niger, Zamfara, Kaduna, and Gombe States in Nigeria. Vaccination campaigns continue at some sites in Nigeria for a total of 255,000 people.

Four months later, in spite of the global toll, the number of deaths has remained relatively low. This was due partly to good case management and also because disease transmission was limited by vaccination campaigns launched quickly once epidemic thresholds were met.

A Doctors Without Borders worker vaccinates a child in Africa. The humanitarian organization's four-hundred vaccination teams immunize thousands of people against meningitis every day. (Stuart Price/ AFP/Getty Images)

Intervention in Niger

MSF teams have been working in close partnership with the Ministry of health to treat affected people in three regions (Maradi, Zinder, Dosso) of southern Niger, as well as in the capital, Niamey. They helped staff of local health structures with case definition and patient treatment. They provided training, and donated meningitis

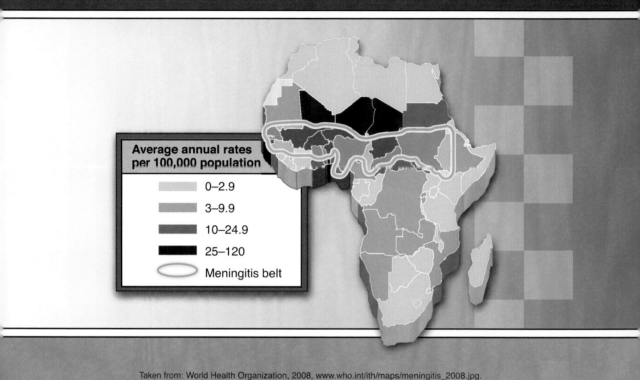

Meningococcal Disease in Africa, 1993–2006

Average annual rates per 100,000 population

- 0–2.9
- 3–9.9
- 10–24.9
- 25–120
- Meningitis belt

Taken from: World Health Organization, 2008, www.who.int/ith/maps/meningitis_2008.jpg.

kits to hospitals and clinics. In parallel with the treatment strategy was a mass vaccination campaign carried out with health ministry workers. 2,838,000 people were vaccinated by MSF and Niger's Ministry of Health.

Zinder: MSF supported health structures for treatment of meningitis patients in six districts of Zinder region. Some 3,300 patients were treated, 148 have died. During the epidemic, a total of 1,510,000 people were vaccinated. MSF teams carried out vaccination campaigns in collaboration with the Ministry of Health for 1,316,000 people in the districts of Matameye, Zinder town, Mirriah, Magaria Tanout, and Goure. Vaccination is now over but a small team is doing follow-up for 2 weeks. Regular activities (nutritional programs) are on-going.

Maradi: Some 1,954 people with meningitis have been reported in the region by the Ministry of Health since the beginning of the year, among whom 63 died. In total, 1,117,410 people were vaccinated. MSF teams carried out vaccination campaigns, in collaboration with the Ministry of Health, in the districts of Maradi city, Madarounfa, Tessaoua, and Aguié and also in Tibiri health center in Guidam Roumji district and at eight health centers in Mayahi district. This represents 851,288 among the people vaccinated. In these areas, on average 92 percent of the target population (aged 2 to 30) has been immunized. The emergency intervention is now over and regular activities (medical and nutritional) are ongoing.

Dosso: A total of 1,745 patients were treated and 102 died during MSF's emergency intervention in this region (between weeks 11 to 18). MSF carried out a vaccination campaign with the Ministry of Heath in Dosso, Doutchi, and Boboye districts. Some 671,266 people were vaccinated. A total of 2,111 daily workers, 38 MSF local staff and around 26 expats were mobilized for this intervention.

Niamey: In the capital of Niger, MSF supported local health structures to treat meningitis patients. Some 285 cases, including 24 deaths, were recorded since the beginning of the year.

Intervention in Nigeria

After many weeks of scaling up, MSF started to close down its activities and the vaccination campaigns are over in most of the nine northern states where it has worked since the end of January. Teams will remain in place for a few more weeks to continue case management and patient treatment in Kebbi State, Sokoto, Niger, Zamfara, Katsina, Jigawa, and Bauchi. Activities are finished in Gombe and Kaduna States. Joint Ministry of

Health and MSF surveillance teams have so far recorded 57,795 cases, along with 1,795 deaths among a population of 38 million.

In parallel with the treatment strategy, vaccination campaigns were carried out by MSF teams with health ministry workers. So far, 4,541,000 people have been vaccinated in nine states where MSF worked with the Ministry of Health. Vaccination is ongoing for 255,000 people. At the end of the intervention, almost 4.8 million people will have been vaccinated by MSF/Ministry of Health in Nigeria during this epidemic.

Intervention in Chad

A total of 1,204 meningitis cases and 133 deaths have been recorded by Chad's Ministry of Health. MSF supported health structures for meningitis treatment in some districts where the epidemic threshold had been reached and in the capital N'Djamena. Some 106,000 people were vaccinated by MSF jointly with the Ministry of Health in Durbali, Pala, and Goundi districts.

CHAPTER 2

Issues Concerning Meningitis

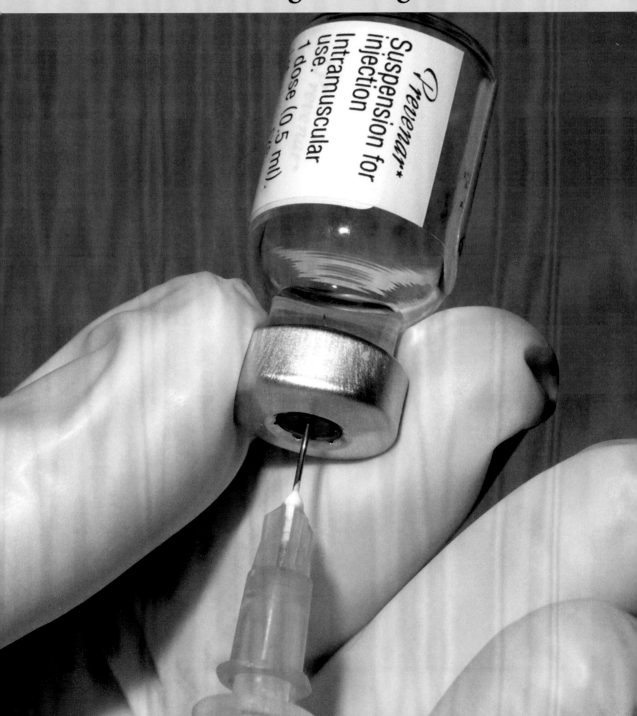

Vaccination of College Students Against Meningitis Is Controversial

Elizabeth F. Farrell

In the following article Elizabeth F. Farrell explains that many states are passing laws mandating vaccination against meningitis for college students, but that this trend is opposed by some campus health officials. It imposes too great a burden on the college, they say, and the incidence of meningitis is rare. Furthermore, the vaccine protects against only four of the five types of bacterial meningitis, and vaccinated students might be less vigilant about meningitis symptoms, believing they are protected when they are not. But advocates for the vaccine believe that because the disease is so serious, even a vaccination that protects only a few people is nevertheless worthwhile. Farrell is a staff writer for the *Chronicle of Higher Education*.

One morning six years ago [in 1998], Ryan N. Pike, a sophomore at Indiana University at Bloomington, woke up with a headache and slight nausea. After attending his morning class, he dragged himself

Photo on previous page. Imposing mandatory vaccinations for meningitis is a controversial issue. (Dr. P. Marazzi/ Photo Researchers, Inc.)

back to bed and slept until 6 P.M. When he awoke, he realized that he had something much worse than the flu.

He was dehydrated. When he tried to sit up in bed, he lost his vision. Purple pinpoint dots covered his arms and legs.

After his parents took him to a hospital that night, doctors diagnosed Mr. Pike with meningococcal meningitis, a severe and rapidly advancing form of bacterial meningitis, which infects the lining of the brain and spinal cord. They gave him antibiotics but told his parents that he had only a 30-percent chance of survival. A priest from the family's parish church gave him last rites.

Gangrene, caused by restricted blood flow, crept into Mr. Pike's limbs and hardened his toes, forcing doctors to amputate nine of them, along with most of his right foot.

After more than six weeks in bed, Mr. Pike recovered. When he returned to Indiana to complete his degree, he began to study the disease that had hit him so suddenly, one that he had not even known existed. He learned that he was lucky to have lived after waiting so long to see a doctor. In cases of meningitis, a few hours can mean the difference between two legs and none, or between life and death.

He learned that the disease is spread through saliva and can be transmitted through coughing, sneezing, shared drinks, or any other form of close contact. Most people who become infected, however, don't contract meningitis and aren't even aware that they are carriers. He also discovered that there is a vaccine that might have prevented him from catching the disease.

Nonprofit Advocacy Groups

After graduating, in December 2001, he accepted a job as development director for the Meningitis Foundation of America, a nonprofit advocacy group focused on increasing awareness of all types of meningitis. The foundation, formed in 1997, and the National Meningitis Association, founded in 2000, are run by volunteers and paid staff members, many of whom are meningitis survivors or family members of meningitis victims.

In their short histories, both groups have proved effective at persuading states to establish laws requiring either vaccinations for college students or informational programs about the disease and the vaccine, Menomune. Since May 2000, 25 states have passed such laws, and similar bills are pending in six other states. Two members of Congress have proposed national legislation.

New Jersey and Connecticut require the vaccination for students living in campus housing at both public and private colleges. But most of the state laws allow students to waive the vaccination by signing a form stating that they have read information about the disease provided by their college.

Laws Are Being Questioned

On the surface, the meningitis laws are the swift product of grass-roots efforts to protect college students from a fatal disease. But many college health officials are questioning whether the laws are necessary. These officials argue that legislators have acted irrationally in response to lobbying efforts by pharmaceutical companies and emotional appeals from small groups of advocates. Some doctors and nurses who treat college students say that the laws place an unnecessary burden on campus medical facilities, and that their own time would be better spent dealing with the more widespread health needs of students.

"We would have to spend time tracking and blocking enrollment [based on waiver signatures] instead of providing direct patient care" to comply with a waiver law, says Peter S. Dietrich, medical director of University Health Services at the University of California at Berkeley. In 2001, California passed a law that requires public colleges to provide information about meningitis and the vaccine to their students, but does not require families to sign waivers.

"In lean times," Dr. Dietrich says, "we have to ask how much we want to chase paper for a relatively rare disease when you have to treat fractures every day and appendicitis at least once a week. It's a judgment call, because people can die from appendicitis if you don't have enough staff to recognize it right away."

Emotional Appeal

What do statistics say about the threat of meningitis?

In the late 1990s, researchers began to track the incidence of the disease among college students. By 2000, the federal Centers for Disease Control and Prevention [CDC] had analyzed the studies and concluded that freshmen living in dormitories, compared with the rest of the population their age, were at a "moderately increased risk" of contracting the disease. Yet the study also showed that the rate of meningitis among college students overall was less than the rate for 18- to 23-year-olds who were not in college.

Various studies have found that the incidence of meningitis among 15-to-24-year-olds more than doubled from 1991 to 1997, from about 0.9 cases to 2.1 cases per 100,000. Yet the disease still affects only a small percentage of students relative to the overall college population: Roughly 125 college students contract meningitis each year, and 5 to 15 of them die. Another 12 to 20 suffer permanent hearing loss, brain damage, and loss of limbs.

"There are just these awful stories that come before legislators, and they're always very moving stories about young, healthy people in the prime of their lives, and it's very sad," says James C. Turner, director of student health at the University of Virginia.

FAST FACT

Although vaccination against meningococcal disease is recommended for travelers of all ages, it is not mandatory for travel to any country except Saudi Arabia, where travelers to Mecca during the annual hajj pilgrimage must have proof of vaccination.

Dr. Turner, who is chairman of the American College Health Association's vaccine committee, says that while 15 deaths per year "is not that many," the tragic nature of the disease overshadows the statistics. "Legislators probably become a little overzealous," he says. "They don't look at the scientific side as much."

Mandatory Vaccination Is Controversial

It is "hard to say to a parent, 'Oh, I'm sorry this happened to your child, but I don't support mandating [vaccination laws] across the country,'" says Reginald Fennel, president of the college-health association.

Neither the college-health group nor the CDC has chosen to support waiver rules. Both organizations make

Lynn Bozof, founder of the National Meningitis Association, poses with a photo of her twenty-year-old son, who died of meningitis. She has been instrumental in instituting mandatory vaccinations for college students in Georgia. (**AP Images**)

only a general recommendation that college students and their parents be informed of the disease and the potential benefits of vaccination.

But Lynn Bozof, founder of the National Meningitis Association, believes that many meningitis deaths could be prevented through vaccines and education on college campuses. She watched five years ago as her 20-year-old son, a pre-med honors student and star baseball player at Georgia Southwestern University, lost both his arms and legs during a 26-day battle with meningitis before succumbing to the disease.

Only after her son's death did Ms. Bozof learn that there was a vaccine that might have kept him from getting sick. The discovery inspired her to found the group, which she says was "instrumental" in persuading lawmakers in her state to adopt a law requiring college students to receive the vaccination or sign a waiver.

"Our mission is to educate parents, students, and even the medical community that this disease is out there," says Ms. Bozof. "I wasn't given any information to make a decision, and I want other parents to have that choice."

No Protection from Type B

Many college health officials question the laws, however, because Menomune, the only meningitis vaccine approved in the United States, does not protect against all strains of the disease.[1] In studies conducted by Aventis Pasteur Limited, which produces the drug, Menomune was at least 90 percent effective in protecting against four of the five main types of bacteria that lead to meningitis.

The vaccine does not, however, provide any protection against the fifth strain, known as Type B, which is responsible for 30- to 40-percent of the cases of bacterial meningitis in the United States, according to Berkeley's Dr. Dietrich.

1. A newer vaccine, Menactra, exists, but it also protects against only four of the five main types of meningitis; it does not protect against type B meningitis.

The CDC has found that 24 percent of the college students who contracted meningitis in 1998 had Type B. The strain also caused the most recent case of meningococcal meningitis among students: Alisa Lewis, a 20-year-old junior at the University of California at Berkeley, died a few hours after being admitted to a hospital with a fever and flu-like symptoms in January, says Dr. Dietrich.

"This is not a great vaccine, because it doesn't cover all types" of meningitis, Dr. Dietrich says. "If there was a better one out there, we might revisit the decision to encourage it, and probably be more proactive about it."

What's more, he said, if students are encouraged to get the vaccine, there is the added risk that some of them will ignore symptoms of meningitis because they assume they are immune to it.

Drug Company's Role

College students' deaths related to alcohol abuse can be as wrenching and sudden as meningitis fatalities, but a big difference between the organizations devoted to discouraging alcohol use and those encouraging meningitis vaccination is financial support from drug companies.

Aventis Pasteur donates about $1.9-million to the National Meningitis Association annually, about 95 percent of the group's operating budget. The company also makes donations to the Meningitis Foundation of America and finances the meningitis-education efforts of the American College Health Association.

In many of the states with meningitis laws, Aventis hired lobbyists to make a case for greater education efforts about the disease and the vaccine.

Len Lavenda, a spokesman for Aventis, says the company's position is consistent with the federal CDC's recommendation that parents and students be informed about meningitis and the availability of a vaccination. The requirement that students sign a statement indicating that they have read information provided by their college about meningitis has led to more of them getting the vaccine, according to a study published in the *Journal of American College Health.*

Although there are no nationwide numbers available on the total increase in vaccines administered on campuses over the past few years, statistics from Brown University are telling: Since the university began mailing brochures to freshmen before their arrival on campus, the proportion of those being vaccinated rose from 13 percent in 1999 to 60 percent in 2001.

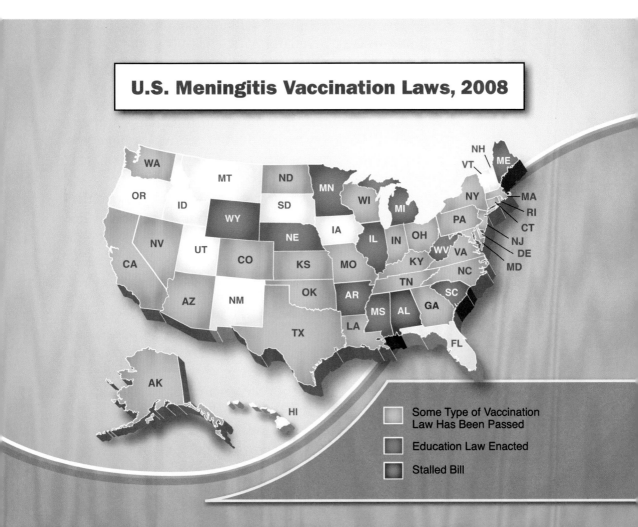

U.S. Meningitis Vaccination Laws, 2008

Some Type of Vaccination Law Has Been Passed

Education Law Enacted

Stalled Bill

Taken from: National Meningitis Association.

The cost of vaccination, $50 to $85 per student, is usually covered by college or independent health-insurance plans. Mr. Lavenda declines to provide sales information on Menomune, saying only that "the meningitis vaccine is one of our smaller-selling vaccines. We're not talking about a huge market or level of sales for us."

Some Say Laws Are Necessary

Ms. Bozof and Mr. Pike, of the anti-meningitis associations, insist that laws requiring signatures for vaccines are necessary because students will not read the information if doing so isn't mandatory. "It ends up in the garbage can, because there's just too much other paperwork" sent by colleges, she says.

Many college health officials, however, say waiver laws are too labor-intensive to enforce. Large universities like Berkeley, with 30,000 students, have too many students to keep track of immunizations, says Dr. Dietrich.

New York's law, which requires all students to either get the vaccine or sign a waiver, even if they don't live on campus, has made for "quite a workload," says Linda MacKenzie, administrative director of health services at the State University of New York at Binghamton.

"There's a lot of programming time spent so we can enter codes and tie [the waiver form] into the registration system," she says. "It's another piece of paperwork that has to be reviewed by a nurse and sent back to the student if it isn't complete."

Recently, the governor of Washington, Gary Locke, a Democrat, reached the same conclusion. When a law on vaccination education and waivers was approved by the Legislature last April, he approved the general-education mandate but vetoed the waiver section, on the grounds that it placed an "unnecessary administrative burden on our higher-education institutions."

"It's Fairly Simple"

Conclusive data on the long-term effect of meningitis-vaccination laws is unlikely to be available for some time. Over the past few years, the number of cases of meningitis at colleges has decreased slightly, but Mr. Lavenda, at Aventis, says that dip could be a function of the natural cycle of the disease's incidence.

In the meantime, some college health providers say campus prevention efforts should focus on what they see as more-pressing health issues, like sexually transmitted diseases and alcohol-related deaths and injuries.

Advocates for anti-meningitis efforts, however, see those problems in a different light. "In my mind, it's a pretty simple difference" between the disease, on the one hand, and alcohol abuse or unprotected sex, on the other, says Mr. Pike, at the Meningitis Foundation of America. "In college, I was able to make choices about that stuff. But I didn't choose to get meningitis."

That distinction reveals one of the main reasons that meningitis laws have won approval in so many states. Unlike other health problems that plague college campuses, meningitis can be contracted regardless of a student's personal habits or moral choices. Instead of getting involved in debates about handing out condoms or controlling access to alcohol, colleges can act to lower the threat of meningitis on their campuses with one seemingly simple requirement.

"When parents are sending their kids off to school, they are looking at ways to reduce risk," says Dr. Turner, at Virginia. "So much of morbidity in college is self-induced, like drinking and driving—and as parents, they can't prevent that. But with this, it's fairly simple. They give them a shot and the risk is reduced."

Support for Mandatory Vaccination Against Meningitis Is Growing

Melissa Dahl

In the following article Melissa Dahl reports that people who have had meningitis and their families favor laws mandating vaccination for teens, since the disease can have terrible consequences. They feel strongly that young people should be required to be vaccinated. However, some others believe that vaccination should not be compulsory. They assert that people should be aware of the risks of side effects before making a decision, and they point out that meningitis is not a common disease. Dahl is a health writer for MSNBC.

Ashley Lee thought it was just the flu coming on. A little headache, an upset stomach—nothing to skip a hometown frat party for, reasoned the 18-year-old as she cruised the 90 miles from Indiana

SOURCE: Melissa Dahl, "Meningitis Threatens College Students," MSNBC, September 5, 2007. www.msnbc.com. Republished with permission of MSNBC.com, conveyed through Copyright Clearance Center, Inc.

University in Bloomington back home to Terre Haute, [Indiana].

But at the party, the college freshman ran to the bathroom to vomit every half hour and eventually headed home, where her parents figured she'd feel better after a good night's sleep. The next day, she collapsed on her way to the bathroom. Her dad carried her to their car, and they sped toward the local hospital. At the emergency room, she lost her vision for several terrifying seconds.

"That scared me half to death," Ashley says. "I knew something wasn't right."

Hours later, Ashley was diagnosed with meningococcal meningitis, a rare but potentially deadly bacterial infection.

The doctor's words hit Ashley's stepmom with a sickening thud. Sam Lee had taken her daughter to the doctor just six weeks earlier to get vaccinated against this very disease before sending her off to college. The doctor didn't have it in stock right then. It's such a rare disease, though, he had said, that Ashley could just get the shot once she got to campus.

Statistically speaking, the doctor was right. Meningococcal meningitis strikes fewer than 3,000 people in the United States each year, many of them college students or children under age 1. But while the bacterial infection is relatively rare, it's also deadly, killing 10 to 12 percent of those it infects, sometimes within hours. The disease attacks and shuts down major organs and prevents blood from circulating to limbs, causing tissue to die. Among survivors, 20 percent suffer brain damage, kidney disease, loss of hearing or sight, limb amputations or other severe complications.

The disease is spread through air droplets and direct contact with someone who is infected. College students, particularly freshmen living in dorms, are at increased risk because of their lifestyle. They're living away from home for the first time and many share everything from drinks to drags off each others' cigarettes. And too many late nights of studying and partying can leave their immune systems run-down and vulnerable.

During her first weeks of college in 2005, Ashley was too busy with new friends and a full class schedule to seek out the vaccine, and it didn't seem like a big deal anyway.

"I just didn't know the severity of it. I thought it was just, like, another vaccination," Ashley recalls.

It wasn't until Ashley's dad told her that the doctors were going to have to take her left foot that she truly understood what meningitis meant.

Life and Death Debate

After the disease attacked Ashley, each of her family members was vaccinated with Menactra, which is approved by the Food and Drug Administration for those ages 11 and older. [It is now also approved for ages 2 to 10.] It's 83 percent effective in preventing four of the five strands of bacterial meningitis.

"Why would you take the chance?" says Sam Lee.

That's a question that has sparked a national debate.

Twenty states now require college students to either get the vaccination or sign a waiver that says they've read about the disease. Three more states mandate the vaccination for college students, but allow exemptions for religious or medical reasons. Eleven states require only that information about the vaccine and the disease be provided on campus.

A growing grassroots movement is pushing for more states to require the shot. Currently, the Centers for Disease Control and Prevention [CDC] recommends Menactra for kids ages 11 to 18, but only 12 percent of teenagers got the vaccine in 2006.

Many of those advocating for mandatory vaccinations are parents, including Frankie Milley, who have lost children to meningitis. Nine years ago [1998], her 18-year-old son, Ryan, died of the disease, and since then, she has

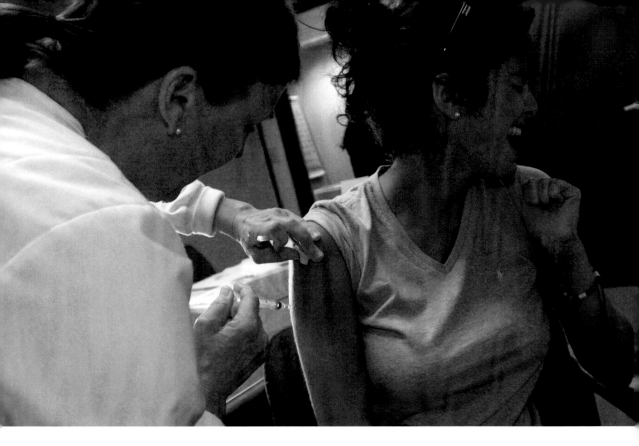

worked in her home state of Texas to make meningitis education available to all families. She also supported a bill currently being considered by the Texas Legislature that would require college students to get the vaccine.

After visiting her son's grave recently, Milley wept during a phone interview. Her memories of her only child are intertwined with regret and anger. When Ryan was alive, she wasn't aware of the vaccination that could have prevented the disease that killed him.

"The hardest thing was to walk to the cemetery, to see his name on a gravestone," Milley says. "His name shouldn't be on a gravestone. It should be on a wedding invitation, a birth announcement. . . . If he'd had that vaccine he wouldn't be there."

Dr. Jim Turner, the executive director for the department of student health at the University of Virginia, was skeptical in 2001 when Virginia passed a law mandating that all students attending four-year universities must get

A University of Maryland student receives a meningitis vaccination as part of the school's mandatory immunization program. (Michael Connor/The Washington Times/ Landov)

the vaccination or sign a waiver. He thought most students would just choose to sign the waiver. But it seems that education about the disease has motivated many to get the vaccine. He's seen the numbers climb from 55 percent of students getting vaccinated to 95 percent.

"It's a safe vaccination, it's an effective vaccination, and it's one of those terrible, terrible risks—albeit extremely rare—that you can really minimize by spending money on the vaccine," says Turner, who is also the chair of the Vaccines Preventable Diseases Committee for the American College Health Association [ACHA]. The vaccine is generally covered by insurance and costs around $120 on most college campuses.

Families Should Know the Risks of Vaccination

Others believe parents should be able to choose which vaccinations they—or their children—receive. Education about the vaccination is vital, but families should know the risks and be able to make their own decisions, says Dr. John Dorman, a committee member of that same ACHA committee and a clinical professor of medicine at Stanford University.

Like any vaccine, Menactra may carry side effects such as allergic reaction and redness or pain around the injected area, according to the CDC. Menactra has also been linked to a few cases of Guillain-Barre syndrome, which attacks the peripheral nervous system and causes gradual, temporary paralysis. Data from the Vaccine Adverse Event Reporting System suggests this happens 1.25 times for every 1 million meningitis vaccines given.

Barbara Loe Fisher, president and co-founder of the National Vaccine Information Center, believes more attention should be drawn to these potential hazards. Her Washington, D.C.–based nonprofit works on the prevention of injuries and deaths caused by vaccinations.

"I just don't understand why we have to force people," Fisher says. "We should make [vaccinations] available at low or no cost, but forcing people is another issue."

A Rare Disease

Those opposed to a mandatory meningitis vaccination also cite the low occurrence of the disease in the United States.

"I guess I err on the side of wanting to make mandatory those things of major public health significance,"

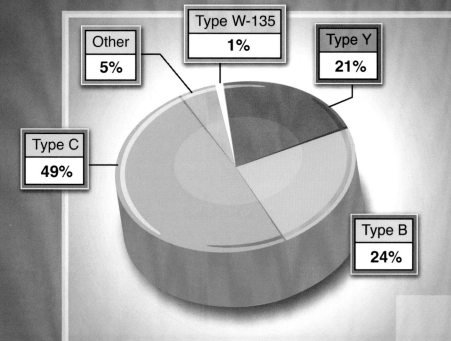

Main Types of Meningococcal Disease in the United States

Types A, B, C, Y, and W-135 cause at least 95 percent of meningococcal disease in the United States.

Other 5%

Type W-135 1%

Type Y 21%

Type C 49%

Type B 24%

Taken from: National Meningitis Association/Centers for Disease Control and Prevention, 2002–2009.

Dorman says. "(Meningitis) isn't a particularly common phenomenon."

But the disease can be horrific when it does strike.

When Lynn Bozof's son Evan was a teenager, there was a meningitis outbreak in a neighboring county. Evan was worried, and he asked his mom if he should get the vaccination.

"'Mom, how do I know if I've got meningitis?'" Bozof recalls her son asking. And she remembers her reply: "Oh Evan, you don't need to worry about meningitis!"

But five years later, as a junior at Georgia Southwestern University in 1998, Evan called his mom complaining of a migraine. It got so bad that he went to the emergency room, where he was diagnosed with meningitis and placed in intensive care. His kidneys shut down. His liver stopped functioning. Both arms and legs had to be amputated. After a 26-day fight against the disease, Evan died.

As Bozof watched her son's losing battle, the memory of a teenage Evan asking about meningitis cruelly replayed in her mind.

"I feel like that came back to haunt me because I didn't take the time to find out about the disease," Bozof says. "Just because this disease is rare doesn't mean it's not going to affect you or someone you know."

"It Happens So Quickly"

The disease's hard-to-spot symptoms and rapid progression make meningococcal meningitis a "great fear" for doctors, says Dr. Tom Clark, a medical epidemiologist for the CDC's National Center for Immunization and Respiratory Diseases. The symptoms are devastatingly easy to overlook, to dismiss as something minor. The only way to definitively diagnose meningococcal meningitis is through a spinal tap, he says, something not routinely done on people who have flulike symptoms.

In Ashley's case, the doctors at first assumed she was merely dehydrated and tried to send her home, the family remembers. Even after a purplish rash—a classic sign of meningitis—spread across her body, emergency-room staff still had no idea what was wrong.

Terrified for his daughter, Ashley's dad, Tom, demanded that she be transferred to a larger hospital. Ashley screamed in pain the entire time it took the ambulance to get to the hospital in Indianapolis, 77 miles away.

"It was a ride from hell," Ashley recalls. "Now that I know about the disease, I could almost feel the disease running through my body, just eating at me."

When she reached the second hospital, a doctor recognized the disease for what it was. By that time, Ashley's parents say her whole body had swelled to twice its normal size, and the purple rash now covered her head to toe. The disease had taken only a little over an hour to overtake her entire body.

"It's not unusual to hear a story of a kid not feeling well on a Friday night and going to bed, and being dead on Saturday morning," says the CDC's Clark. "It happens so quickly."

Lingering Effects

Even when a victim survives meningitis, the nightmarish battle against the disease is far from over.

As Ashley fought for her life in the hospital, she and her father made the devastating decision to let her doctors take her left foot and three of her fingers.

They talked about it at length and cried about Ashley's loss. But when she woke up hours later, she had no memory of that conversation.

"She'd wake up after each surgery and say, 'Dad, what happened to my foot?'" Tom Lee remembers. Brokenhearted, he would tell her again.

Now, two years after she got sick, 20-year-old Ashley's right arm is scarred from skin grafts and she wears a prosthetic foot. Her other leg is in a cast, following the latest of 11 surgeries.

At home in her bedroom painted two shades of pink, pictures of her physical therapists sit among those of her friends and family. At first the therapists were skeptical about whether she'd be able to walk at all. But Ashley was determined to get back on her feet. Despite pain from the recent surgery and a pronounced limp, she refuses to even use a cane for support, walking instead entirely on her own.

Ashley spent last summer covering up the lasting marks of meningitis. Despite the sweaty, humid Indiana summer, she wore shrugs and pants to keep people from seeing her scars. But the following year when she returned to school, she made a series of bold moves: She put on a tank top. She had her seven remaining fingers professionally manicured. And she started to tell her story.

She feels as if it's her responsibility to educate people about the devastating effects of meningitis and to urge others to get the vaccine. She works closely with the National Meningitis Association and has appeared in an informational video the nonprofit group produced. On campus, where she's majoring in biology in hopes of going to medical school, she plays the video and speaks to classes about her experience. And she's fielded technical questions about her condition from crowds of doctors and researchers.

"It helps me; it's kind of like therapy for myself," Ashley says.

She and her family still get angry at times, thinking about the vaccination that she nearly received, the vaccination that could have prevented all this. But she keeps her dad's advice in mind: Every day we have a choice, he says. Either look forward, or look back.

FAST FACT

Meningitis B and C together are the most prevalent types in the Americas and Europe, whereas meningitis A accounts for most cases in Africa and Asia.

But telling her story over and over again can be draining for Ashley. Every time she walks a stranger through her story for the first time, she has to relive the pain, the ambulance ride, the surgeries and every detail of her nightmarish experience yet again. But it's worth it, she says, "even if I can save just one person."

All Adolescents Should Be Vaccinated Against Meningitis

Melinda Beck

In the following article Melinda Beck points out the terrible results of meningococcal meningitis and argues that the disease can be largely prevented by the new vaccine Menactra. Yet as of 2006, she says, only 12 percent of eleven- to eighteen-year-olds had received the vaccine, partly because parents forget to take adolescents to the doctor for regular checkups and the vaccine is not required. Few people knew of the older vaccine, Menomune, which was not as effective and did not last as long. Menactra will last through the college years even if received at age one, and Beck asserts that it is a safe vaccine despite rare side effects. Beck is a columnist for the *Wall Street Journal*, writing the weekly Health Journal column and related features.

The stories sound chillingly similar. A healthy teenager comes down with what seems like the flu, then gets rapidly weaker, spikes a high fever, starts

SOURCE: Melinda Beck, "Quelling a Killer: The Case for the Meningococcal Vaccine," *Wall Street Journal*, August 5, 2008. Copyright © 2008 by Dow Jones & Company. Republished with permission of Dow Jones & Company, conveyed through Copyright Clearance Center, Inc.

vomiting and breaks out in a rash. By the time he or she gets to the hospital, infection is overwhelming the body's defenses and shutting down vital organs.

David Pasick, a 13-year-old in Wall Township, N.J., was dead in less than 24 hours. Evan Bozof, a Georgia college student, lingered for 26 days while doctors amputated all four limbs in a futile attempt to save him.

Meningococcal meningitis strikes just 1,400 to 2,800 Americans a year—but with terrifying speed and consequences. Roughly 10% of victims die, often hours after symptoms set in. About 15% of those who survive are left with brain damage, hearing loss or amputations; gangrene sets in rapidly if the disease disrupts blood flow to the limbs. Many victims are adolescents and college kids living away from home for the first time.

As a new TV ad points out, the disease is largely preventable with a vaccine called Menactra, licensed in the U.S. in 2005. The Centers for Disease Control and Prevention [CDC] now recommends Menactra for all 11- to 18-year-olds. As of 2006, however, only 12% of those eligible had received the vaccine. Sanofi Pasteur, the manufacturer, expects the rate to rise to 50% this year [2008]. Even so, that leaves tens of millions of teenagers unprotected.

FAST FACT

Intimate kissing is a risk factor for meningococcal meningitis in adolescents, according to the results of a population-based study reported in February 2006 by the *British Medical Journal*.

That's partly because adolescents tend to steer clear of the doctor's office. "Parents are supposed to take their child to the pediatrician every year, and that happens till they're about age six," says Carol J. Baker, a professor of pediatrics at Baylor College of Medicine in Houston. "Then parents start forgetting. Pediatricians don't nag them and schools don't require it."

Adolescents Need to Be Educated

The CDC is pushing the idea of an adolescent doctor visit to discuss a range of health issues as well as get

Only about 12 percent of adolescents in the United States get vaccinated against meningitis, even though the vaccine is readily available. (Mike Simons/Getty Images)

the meningitis vaccine, a diphtheria-tetanus-pertussis booster and the human papilloma virus [HPV] shot for girls. But unlike infants and toddlers, who don't have much say in their vaccines, "adolescents often need to be educated about the need," says Dr. Baker.

Starting this fall [2008], New Jersey will require sixth graders to be vaccinated against meningococcal meningitis. Other states require college students to be vaccinated or sign a waiver saying that they have been informed and opted not to have it.

About 15% to 20% of the population carries the meningococcal bacterium without having any symptoms. But such carriers can transmit it to people who are more susceptible, via sneezing, coughing, kissing or sharing drinks or cigarettes. That's why the disease often hits people living in close quarters like college dorms and sleep-away camps. Teens who are run down and sleep-deprived are especially vulnerable, and the lack of supervision means that symptoms aren't always recognized early.

PERSPECTIVES ON DISEASES AND DISORDERS

"A parent would have that gut instinct that this isn't a simple flu—but a sorority sister or a roommate might not realize it," says Katherine Karlsrud, a New York City pediatrician.

Minutes Count

"Minutes count," notes Candie Benn of San Diego, whose daughter, Melanie, came down with the disease on Christmas Eve in 1995 during her freshman year in college. "We got her to the hospital in 40 minutes and her veins were collapsing. I was still thinking she had the flu and they're telling me she has a 50% chance of living," Ms. Benn says. Melanie survived—but only after three months in intensive care with skin grafts, two months of rehab, a kidney transplant and amputations of both legs and arms.

The Benns and other families were devastated to learn, too late, that there was a vaccine against meningococcal meningitis available even in the 1990s, called Menomune, that might have saved their children. But it wasn't as effective as the new version and few people knew of it or that meningococcal meningitis was such a threat. Several families banded together in 2002 to form the National Meningitis Association, www.nmaus.org, which works to spread awareness both of the disease and the vaccine, funded in part by Sanofi.

"My son was an honor student, pre-med, gorgeous, happy," says Evan's mother, Lynn Bozof, the association's executive director. "We went through 26 days where we saw his hands and feet turn black as the gangrene set in. He lost his kidney function and his liver function and had 10 hours of Grand Mal seizures, and to think that all this could have been prevented with a vaccine that we just didn't know about. That's why it's so important to get the message out now."

Menactra Lasts Eight to Ten Years

Menactra lasts eight to ten years, long enough to take even 11 year olds through the high-risk early college

Meningitis Cases by Age, 2003

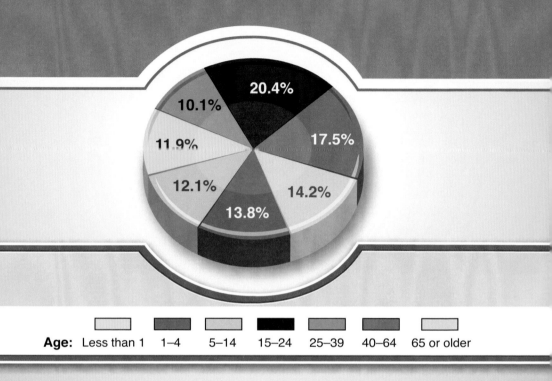

20.4%

10.1%

11.9%

12.1%

13.8%

14.2%

17.5%

Age: Less than 1   1–4   5–14   15–24   25–39   40–64   65 or older

Taken from: MSNBC, "New Meningitis Shots Urged for Kids," May 26, 2005.

years. (The incidence of meningococcal meningitis drops by about half, to about 1 case in 200,000, in adults, so the CDC does not recommend the vaccine for them as well.) It protects against four of the five strains of meningococcal meningitis, which account for 70% of cases in the U.S. It's not made with live virus, so there is no danger of getting the disease from the shot, nor does it contain the preservative thimerosal. The injection costs $80 to $100, but is covered by most insurers. Side effects are minimal. Some people have pain and swelling at the injection site, and a handful have come down with Guillain-Barre syndrome (GBS), a neurological disorder, after receiving Menactra. People who have been diagnosed with GBS are advised not to get Menactra.

That worries some vaccine critics, particularly when Menactra and the HPV vaccine are given together. "This [is] the first time we have ever given adolescents multiple vaccines. Where are the studies that look at whether or not this is a healthy thing to do over the long term?" asks Barbara Loe Fisher, co-founder of the National Vaccine Information Center, a nonprofit activist group. She notes that the U.S. government now recommends 69 doses of 16 different vaccines for kids between 12 hours and 18 years old—triple the number in the 1980s.

Paul Offit, chief of infectious diseases at Children's Hospital in Philadelphia, says that even if a link to GBS were proven, "you have a 20-fold greater chance of getting meningococcal meningitis without the vaccine than of getting GBS from the vaccine, and even if you get GBS, you'll likely recover. . . . Statistically, the choice is very clear."

Getting vaccinated "isn't always at the top of people's priorities, or kids say, 'oooh, I don't like shots,'" says Melanie Benn, now 31 and a social worker. "But people need to know that this exists and, by the way, you can prevent it."

Vaccination Against Meningitis Should Not Be Mandatory

Olivia Wang

In the following viewpoint Olivia Wang, a student at Yale University, argues against requiring college students to be vaccinated against meningitis. She states that the disease is not as deadly and widespread as the media have claimed; in Connecticut there are only one or two vaccine-preventable cases per year. In addition, she asserts, vaccination may not prevent getting the disease, and so it may give people a false sense of security. Furthermore, Wang argues, to require vaccination as a condition of getting on-campus housing violates the right of students to make personal decisions.

"Please stop and read this email! Connecticut state law now requires students living in on-campus housing to be vaccinated with the Meningococcal (Meningitis) vaccine." Just a few days after coming back from winter break [in 2002], all Yale College students received this notice announcing the new Connecticut state

SOURCE: Olivia Wang, "Vaccine Ill-Conceived, Rights Violation," *Yale Herald*, vol. XXXIII, February 1, 2002. © 2002 The Yale Herald. Reproduced by permission.

health policy regarding meningitis vaccination. The law is the result of public fears over meningitis, following a 1993 outbreak at the University of Connecticut.

At first glance, this may seem like a generous health measure initiated by the state of Connecticut on behalf of its students. A medical vaccination prevents the spread of an infectious disease; a state-mandated vaccination as a condition of campus residence benefits the students living in close quarters; the greater interest of public health and security is served. Upon closer analysis, however, the new Connecticut state law carries implications that should be considered seriously by students and parents alike.

Vaccination May Not Prevent Many Cases

The first consideration is obtaining an accurate understanding of the scope and nature of the meningococcal disease. Two forms exist: viral (aseptic) and bacterial meningitis, caused by the bacterium *Neisseria meningitidis*. Symptoms include fever, severe headache, nausea, rash, inflammation of the throat and ear, and lethargy. In both viral and bacterial cases, the illness can be serious but is rarely fatal in healthy persons. Contrary to media portrayal of meningitis as an extremely deadly and widespread health threat, the Connecticut State Health Department estimated that the number of vaccine-preventable cases in the state each year amounted to only one or two. Getting a vaccination may not actually prevent the contraction of meningitis, and may provide a false sense of security. While the Department views vaccination as a preventative health measure, it rightly questions the cost-effectiveness of a mandated vaccine.

The Centers for Disease Control and Prevention [CDC] are also skeptical of a mass vaccination program.

> **FAST FACT**
>
> According to the Meningitis Research Foundation of Canada, 10 to 20 percent of adolescents and adults carry the meningococcus bacteria in the back of their noses and throats without any noticeable effects. Only one or two in one hundred thousand have severe meningococcal infections.

Students at Yale College must get vaccinated against meningitis to qualify for on-campus housing. Some argue that this requirement violates students' rights. (**Antonia Reeve/ Photo Researchers**, Inc.)

Their Advisory Committee on Immunization Practices (ACIP) concedes that college freshmen are at "modestly increased risk" to the disease relative to people outside of a college or university environment. However, education—not vaccination—is what the ACIP recommends in order for students and parents "to make individualized, informed decisions regarding vaccination."[1] In a Connecticut Department of Health Fact Sheet on the disease, the government acknowledges that the "vaccination . . . is not universally recommended by all health authorities. Your decision to accept the vaccine is a personal one."

1. The CDC has since changed its policy and recommends that everyone between ages eleven and eighteen be vaccinated.

Percentage of Subjects Aged 11–18 Reporting Adverse Reactions to the Menactra Meningitis Vaccine

Reaction within 7 days	Number of Subjects = 2,264		
	Any	Moderate	Severe
Redness	10.9	1.6	0.6
Swelling	10.8	1.9	0.5
Induration (hardening of soft tissue)	15.7	2.5	0.3
Pain	59.2	12.8	0.3
Headache	35.6	9.6	1.1
Fatigue	30.0	7.5	1.1
Malaise (feeling unwell)	21.9	5.8	1.1
Arthralgia (joint pain)	17.4	3.6	0.4
Diarrhea	12.0	1.6	0.3
Anorexia	10.7	2.0	0.3
Chills	7.0	1.7	0.2
Fever	5.1	0.6	0.0
Vomiting	1.9	0.4	0.3
Rash	1.6		
Seizure	0.0		

Taken from: Product Information for Menactra, Sanofi Pasteur, April 2008.

Vaccination Law Violates Rights

Not any more. The new state legislation, while implementing a preventive health measure, violates the personal right of a student to decide on meningitis vaccination and imposes a consequence based on a negative decision: no housing. This mandatory measure eliminates personal choice on many different levels, because students *must* comply with the vaccination procedure, or else they are barred from on-campus housing. The medical and social benefits of vaccinations against an infectious disease are well known and documented; however, the basis for a state-mandated meningitis vaccination is unclear. The statistics seem to differ from popular belief about the exact scope and nature of meningitis. Given these factors, educational programs about meningitis on university campuses might be an effective alternative and tool for disseminating accurate information about the disease.

Am I afraid of contracting meningitis? Yes. Do I want to infect others around me with meningitis? No. Am I going to get the vaccination? No. Once again, the decision is no longer a personal one.

Steroids Should Be Given to Patients with Bacterial Meningitis

Zahra Ahmadinejad et al.

In the following article four doctors from Tehran University of Medical Sciences, Zahra Ahmadinejad, Vahid Ziaee, Masood Aghsaeifar, and Seied Reza Reiskarami, discuss a study in which they examined the clinical, laboratory, neuroimaging, and therapeutic factors associated with mortality in patients with meningitis. Although admitting the use of steroids for treatment of meningitis is still debated, they argue that the use of adjunctive corticosteroid therapy played an important role in the recovery of the patients. The lack of the use of a steroid was associated with a high mortality rate. Therefore, they suggest that an early diagnosis, use of antibiotics, and steroid therapy are all important factors in recovery.

The World Health Organization (WHO) estimates that one third of the world's population is infected with mycobacterium tuberculosis, with the highest prevalence of tuberculosis in Asia. Tuberculous meningitis (TBM) is one of the most common clinical

SOURCE: Internet Journal of Infectious Diseases, vol. 3, 2003. Reproduced by permission.

and morphological [anatomical] manifestations of extrapulmonary tuberculosis and remains a serious health threat in developing countries.

Combating a High Mortality Rate

However, despite . . . the advent of the newer antituberculosis drugs and modern imaging techniques, mortality and morbidity remains high. Most studies [have] suggested that [a] combination of various factors like delayed diagnosis and treatment, extremes of ages, associated chronic systemic diseases and advanced stage of disease at presentation may contribute to this high morbidity and mortality rate.

In this study, we evaluated certain clinical, laboratory, neuroimaging and therapeutic factors associated with mortality. . . .

Tuberculous diseases are still relatively common in countries such as [those in] the Middle East and southern Asia where the disease is endemic. Tuberculous meningitis is one of the major infectious causes of chronic meningitis worldwide (including Iran), with high mortality and morbidity.

The overall mortality rate in this study was 22%, a figure which is close to the lower limit of the reported mortality rate. The significant prognostic variables derived by univariate analysis in our study included the staging of TBM at admission, the effective treatment of hydrocephalous, age (>10y [less than 10 years]) and corticosteroid therapy. Other studies regarding the prognosis of TBM, which employed univariate analysis, had revealed the important role of age, stage of TBM on admission, mental status and associated extra enhancing exudates on CT scan.

Stage of the TBM on admission indicates the severity of disease. The severity of TBM on admission was a significant prognostic factor with those in stage III having a 32.6% mortality rate, which was in accordance with other reports.

The age of the patients (especially <10y) was a significant prognostic factor in our study. Age has a different role on prognosis of patients with TBM in different studies. In some study [sic], lower age was found to be a good prognostic factor. However the significant association between low age, particularly lower than 5 years and grave prognosis was also noted in other studies. . . .

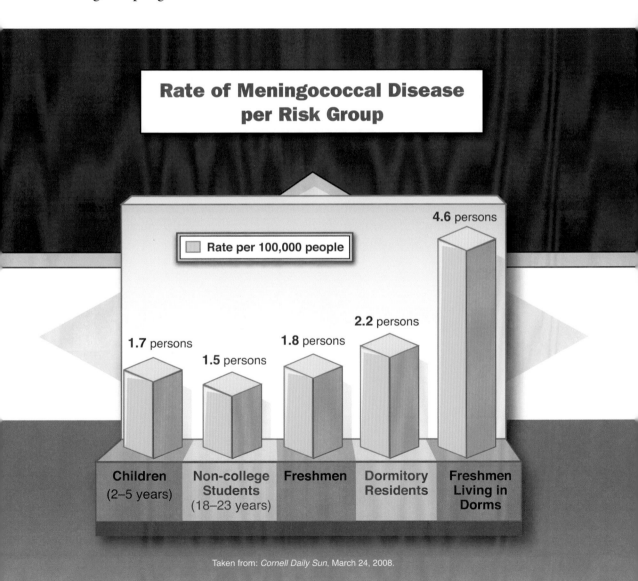

Rate of Meningococcal Disease per Risk Group

Rate per 100,000 people

1.7 persons — Children (2–5 years)

1.5 persons — Non-college Students (18–23 years)

1.8 persons — Freshmen

2.2 persons — Dormitory Residents

4.6 persons — Freshmen Living in Dorms

Taken from: *Cornell Daily Sun*, March 24, 2008.

The Use of Steroids for Treatment of TBM

The routine use of steroids for treatment of TBM is still debated. Some investigators believed that patients presenting with severe disease may benefit from steroid therapy. Their value in reducing cerebral edema and inflammatory exudates and preventing spinal block, particularly in infants, appears to be generally accepted. It is not at all clear that steroid therapy might have a prolonged beneficial clinical effect. However, in our study, adjunctive corticosteroid therapy had a good role on the outcome.

In summary, TBM, a central nervous system infectious disease with high mortality rate, especially in children, is still a serious public health problem. The presence of hydrocephalous, severity of TBM on admission and the lack of adjunctive corticosteroid therapy are strongly associated with mortality rate. Some of the prognostic factors are correctable. Therefore, early diagnosis, early use of antituberculosis treatment, corticosteroid therapy and treatment of the associated complications such as hydrocephalous are mandatory.

Steroids May Not Benefit Children with Bacterial Meningitis

Ed Edelson

In the following article Ed Edelson reports that although steroids are increasingly used to treat children with bacterial meningitis, a recent study has shown that they may not reduce death rates or the length of hospital stays. The study's senior researcher, however, suggests that larger trials must be done to know more. The death rate from bacterial meningitis in children is very low, and the impact of treating with steroids in a small trial is difficult to discern. Also, the study did not consider the effect of steroids, if any, on long-term neurological damage such as hearing loss. The study also did not report at what point in the course of the infection the steroids were given, a detail that could be relevant. Edelson is a reporter for HealthDay.

Corticosteroids are increasingly used to help treat children with bacterial meningitis, but a new study finds that adding the drugs to antibiotic treatment may not reduce death rates or the length of hospital stays.

SOURCE: Ed Edelson, "Corticosteroids of Little Use Against Childhood Meningitis," HealthDay, May 6, 2008. www.healthday .com. Reproduced by permission.

But the study—which involved 2,780 children treated for this potentially lethal infection of tissues lining the brain—isn't the last word on the issue, said senior researcher Dr. Samir S. Shah, an infectious diseases specialist at the Children's Hospital of Philadelphia.

One reason is that the death rate from the infection in children is so low that a real difference is statistically hard to demonstrate, Shah said. Mortality among adults with bacterial meningitis runs as high as 30 percent, while in children "it is quite low, in the 4 to 5 percent range," he said.

So the study results didn't exclude the possibility that a benefit from corticosteroids could exist, Shah said, but "if it does, it is very small."

His team published its findings in the May [2008] issue of the *Journal of the American Medical Association.*

In the study, just 248 of the nearly 2,800 children treated at 27 U.S. pediatric hospitals received corticosteroids, about 9 percent of the total. However, steroid use among youngsters with the illness doubled during the study period—from under 6 percent in 2001 to 12 percent in 2006.

The overall death rate for children getting corticosteroids was 6 percent, compared to 4 percent among those not getting them. Hospital stays averaged 12 days for children getting corticosteroids and 10 days for those not receiving them. Neither difference was statistically significant, meaning this outcome could have happened by chance.

Shah himself pointed out what he saw as a flaw of the study: It did not consider the neurological damage done by meningitis, such as hearing loss. Some studies have indicated that corticosteroid treatment might reduce such damage, he said.

Larger Trial Needed

"The way I would want people to use our study is not to say there does not seem to be a benefit, or that [cortico-

> **FAST FACT**
>
> President Barack Obama's daughter Sasha had meningitis when she was three months old. She has not suffered any lasting effects.

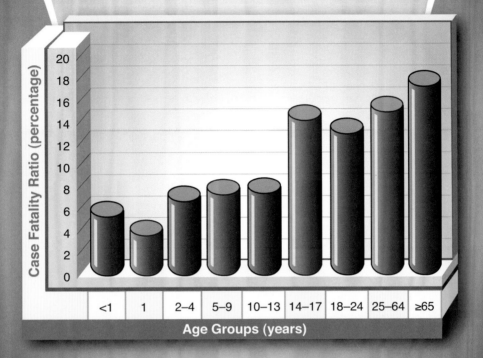

Percentage of Meningitis Fatalities by Age Group, 1991—2002

Case Fatality Ratio (percentage)

20 18 16 14 12 10 8 6 4 2 0

Age Groups (years): <1, 1, 2–4, 5–9, 10–13, 14–17, 18–24, 25–64, ≥65

Taken from: American College Health Association/Centers for Disease Control and Prevention.

steroids] should be used routinely, but to regard it as an impetus for a large, randomized trial," Shah said. "At this point, it would seem that the benefits do not outweigh the risks of using corticosteroids in children, but we need a large-scale clinical trial looking at neurological damage before deciding yes or no."

The study had another flaw, said Dr. Robert W. Frenck, a professor of pediatrics in the division of infectious diseases at Cincinnati Children's Hospital Medical Center: It did not include information on when in the course of the infection corticosteroids were given.

Shown here is a light micrograph of *Haemophilus influenzae* type b bacteria, one of several bacteria that cause meningitis. Vaccines have successfully reduced cases of the disease. (Science Source/Photo Researchers, Inc.)

"A number of studies with animals and humans have shown that using corticosteroids before the first dose of antibiotics has the most benefit," Frenck said. "It reduces the inflammatory response that results when the immune system kills the bacteria."

Physicians who treat meningitis are likely to say that the study supports whatever they are now doing, he said. "If people are in the camp where corticosteroids are not regarded as helpful, they will say this shows that they

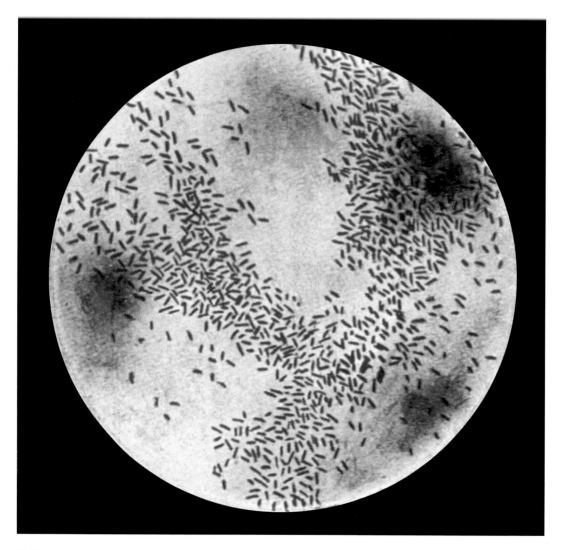

don't help," Frenck said. "If they are in the camp where they are seen as beneficial, they will say that the study does not disprove it."

The large-scale trial proposed by Shah is not likely to happen, Frenck said, and for a cheerful reason—the very low incidence of bacterial meningitis among American children. Vaccines against the bacteria that cause meningitis, such as [*Haemophilus*] *influenzae* type B, have successfully reduced the incidence of the disease, Frenck said. For that reason, bacterial meningitis now occurs in about eight in every 100,000 American children.

"The vaccines have had a tremendous effect," Frenck said. "What you want to do is prevent it."

New Zealand's Mass Meningitis Vaccination Campaign Was Unethical

Barbara Sumner Burstyn and Ron Law

In the following article opponents of a two-year program for vaccinating children against the strain of meningitis B prevalent in New Zealand argue that the New Zealand government, the media, and the public were misled by both officials and scientists. They say that the vaccine was untested and experimental, and that as a result of misconduct on the part of officials, it was not known to be safe or effective. They maintain that the program should be stopped and that its development and implementation should be investigated by a commission of inquiry. Burstyn is a New Zealand writer. Law is an independent risk and policy analyst with many years of experience as a medical laboratory scientist and as a university business management lecturer.

Nﾪew Zealand's meningococcal disease story, as unraveled through analysis of previously secret documents obtained under the Official Information Act, reveals that the New Zealand government,

SOURCE: Barbara Sumner Burstyn and Ron Law, "The Meningococcal Gold Rush," *Scoop*, February 7, 2005. www.scoop.com. Reproduced by permission of the authors.

media and public have been misled and manipulated by officials, advisors and scientists alike.

As a result of this manipulation, the government has committed an unprecedented 200 million taxpayer dollars to a mass vaccination experiment of 1.15 million New Zealand children with an untested and experimental vaccine. Despite being reassured by a bevy of pro-vaccine and vaccine manufacturer sponsored experts and noneless than the Minister of Health herself that the MeNZB™ vaccine is thoroughly tested and proven to be safe and effective, we reveal that Chiron's MeNZB™ vaccine was never used in the trials used to approve its license. We reveal that despite assurances, there is no evidence that the MeNZB™ vaccine will actually work as promised.

We believe that the magnitude of policy, regulatory and scientific misconduct is such that not only should vaccination with this vaccine be halted forthwith, but that the meningococcal vaccination program should be independently audited and the circumstances surrounding the development and implementation of the program subjected to a full Royal Commission of Inquiry.

An Expensive Experiment

In January 2002 the Minister of Health Annette King announced that "$100 million-plus" had been set aside to fund development and implementation of a vaccine to combat New Zealand's unique strain-specific meningococcal group B bacterium.

By May that year, following Ministry of Health negotiations with the preferred contract supplier, Chiron Corporation, that figure had become "a commitment of up to $200 million." By September 2004 the sum of $250 million was being mentioned in parliament.

In a July 7 2004 press release Ms King described the development and approval of the MeNZB™ vaccine as "fantastic news." She went on to explain that the MeNZB™ vaccine had been "specifically developed with scientists

In New Zealand, opponents of using the Chiron Corporation's MeNZB™ vaccine to inject over 1 million children say that the vaccine was untested and experimental. (AP Images)

from biotechnology company Chiron Corporation." Cabinet was told in 2001, immediately prior to approving the signing of the Chiron contract, that the deal included the "development of a unique or 'orphan' vaccine."

Chiron's own press release declared they [Chiron] had specifically developed the vaccine. The company quoted Ms King congratulating them "for their effort and dedication to this project."

But documents received under the Official Information Act reveal that the MeNZB™ vaccine was not developed by Chiron Corporation. It was developed by the Norwegian Institute of Public Health. Chiron had bought the rights to mass manufacture and market the Norwegian meningococcal B vaccines in November 1999, nearly two years before the New Zealand government signed the initial contract with the company. . . .

From the Norwegian perspective, the off-loading of their Norwegian specific vaccine to Chiron must have been a godsend given it had likely invested over a hundred million $US in double blind, placebo controlled studies involving 170,000 people and over 2,000 doctors and nurses for a vaccine that was never licensed for use in mass vaccination. . . .

Inadequate Trials

However the *Lancet* medical journal reported in 1991 that the Norwegian Institute of Public Health found that the large and robust clinical trials proved the vaccine to have insufficient efficacy to justify its use in a mass vaccination program. The *Lancet* paper also contained data showing that the epidemic was waning naturally by the completion of the trials. The incidence had declined from peak levels by about 50%, similar to the natural decline that had occurred in New Zealand when the vaccine was approved. . . .

Of the two trial groups that have been tested with the Chiron produced MeNZB™ vaccine, the minutes of the Minister's MAAC [Medicines Assessment Advisory Committee] vaccine sub-committee noted that one involved a total of ten adults. The number of 8–12 year old children involved in the other group is still unknown, but is unlikely to be more than a handful. . . .

The expert committee's conclusion was that, "the current data supplied provides very limited data on its effectiveness," and "evidence of efficacy is not compelling." They went on to say, "the Committee was concerned that there was no efficacy data for the proposed [MeNZB™] vaccine, and were not convinced that the efficacy and safety monitoring during the roll out was sufficient to maintain public safety and confidence." The Ministry of Health's Dr Jane O'Hallahan has admitted that MeNZB™ vaccine would be rolled out without "efficacy data." . . .

The Minister has refused to release age related deaths for the epidemic strain [of meningococcal disease]. But our best estimates are that the vaccine, if it proves effective, will prevent at most 1 or 2 deaths per year in under 20 year olds out of approximately 700 who die each year from all causes. In other words 0.2% of all deaths in the under 20's might be prevented. Put another way, if the government applied the same cost-benefit analysis to preventing the other 99.8% of deaths, it would be spending over $100 billion.

The numbers game extends to international medical conferences. At the Chiron sponsored, Seventh Annual Conference on Vaccine Research in Virginia, USA in May 2004, the MOH [Ministry of Health] meningococcal vaccine program director, Dr Jane O Hallahan was an invited speaker. Her abstract reads in part, "With the epidemic claiming up to one life every two weeks in a nation of four million people, this collaborative group is working against the clock."

At the time the abstract would have been written, the death rate had fallen to one death every four weeks from all forms of meningococcal disease and one death every three months from the epidemic strain of bacteria.

In another anomaly, in 2001 the Ministry of Health told Cabinet, through a document requesting funding for the Meningococcal B vaccine, that the vaccine would most likely cause herd immunity. "[The preferred] option also has the benefit of likely herd immunity. This is expected but cannot be quantified." The document contains other allusions to expectation of herd immunity. Later in the document the Minister's Office memo categorically stated that herd immunity had been achieved in meningococcal vaccination programs in the United Kingdom and Cuba.

But the United Kingdom program used a Meningococcal C vaccine, and the Cuban study used a B/C com-

FAST FACT

There are large differences in incidence rates of meningococcal disease, both between neighboring countries and within the same country, because of differences in the circulating strains of the bacteria that cause it.

bo, vaccines that are totally different in their make-up. Meningococcal B vaccines cannot be made using the same process as meningococcal C vaccines as they would induce antibodies that attack the brain. It is generally understood to be scientific fraud to compare different entities as if they were the same. . . .

Conflict of Interest

The choice of Chiron Corporation as the exclusive manufacturer of the New Zealand vaccine also raises a number of questions. Cabinet papers show that Ministry officials rejected competitor options and entered into the initial contract with Chiron knowing that Chiron would only produce the vaccine if they got the contracts to both manage the trials and supply the vaccine for the clinical trials and the roll-out. This raises conflict of interest issues as Chiron effectively controlled [whether] or not the government paid it for 3–4 million doses of its vaccine. . . .

Paradoxically, Chiron's publicly stated intentions are to produce a combined meningococcal B and C vaccine. Government papers show that trials have been undertaken in New Zealand using Chiron's meningococcal C vaccine Menjugate™ combined with the Norwegian vaccine.

Chiron's Menjugate™ vaccine was also used as the control in a MeNZB™ trial of infants in New Zealand. The infants were given Menjugate™ vaccine as a so-called "placebo." This fact is not mentioned in the MAAC minutes but was disclosed in a paper presented by Chiron at a scientific conference in Japan in October 2004.

This raises serious questions regarding informed consent. Were parents and guardians aware that Chiron was undertaking what would appear to be unapproved trials of a vaccine that is not licensed for use in New Zealand nor the USA?

In October 2004 Chiron stated that the FDA [U.S. Food and Drug Administration] had requested further information regarding its application to license Menjugate™ in the USA. Since then, Chiron has withdrawn their USA application for approval of Menjugate™ on the premise that they want to introduce a combo vaccine with a broader market appeal. This seems to be a puzzling move, however, given that they had recently completed phase III clinical trials on Menjugate™; it seems odd that if the trial results had been positive that Chiron would not have proceeded with its application.

A Wide Market

So, what are Chiron's motives? Aside from simple commercial opportunism, there is wide market appeal for a New Zealand financed and trialed vaccine. New Zealand's Environmental Science and Research (ESR) annual report this year [2005] commented, "the trials are definitely of international interest because the same strain is now causing problems in Europe, although not yet at an epidemic level. . . . It's of huge international interest." Chiron's competitor Aventis said recently that meningitis B must be the next vaccine target in the US. . . .

Despite all of this, pharmaceutical companies themselves acknowledge that the meningococcal B bacterium is uniquely resistant to vaccination. In fact in 2000 Chiron's Dr Rappuoli stated that, "Conventional research approaches to develop effective vaccines against different strains of group B meningococcus have failed." In 2002 Dr Rappuoli reported that despite years of effort, biomedical scientists failed to find a protective molecule that would induce immunity to type B meningococcal disease.

Perhaps this is why Chiron has recently commenced clinical trials of a genetically engineered broad-spectrum meningococcal B vaccine. This begs the question; is New Zealand's foray into the international vaccine game little more than a form of naive and cynical political manipulation. . . .

The Rise and Fall of Meningococcal Disease in New Zealand

Contrary to assertions by the New Zealand government that meningitis cases were not decreasing, the MeNZB™ vaccine was introduced at a time when case numbers had already declined significantly.

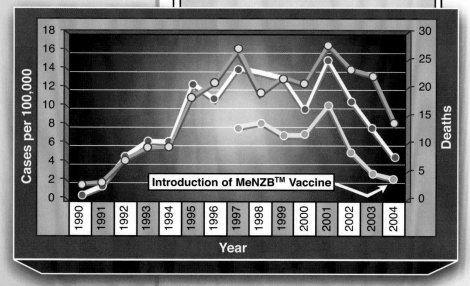

Legend:
- Cases of Total Meningococcal Disease per 100,000
- Total Deaths
- Deaths Due to MeNZB™ Strain

Introduction of MeNZB™ Vaccine

Year (1990–2004)

Taken from: Barbara Sumner Burstyn and Ron Law, "The Meningococcal Gold Rush," Scoop, February 7, 2005.

While Chiron's motives may be transparent, it is the roles of New Zealand researchers and medical regulators that are of primary concern.

Ethical Questions

Numerous countries are beginning to ask about the alliances between science, research, regulators and the pharmaceutical industry and the conflicts of interest those alliances create. Specifically there are significant connections and conflicts of interest between the corporation holding the trademark on the MeNZB™ vaccine and researchers and regulators in New Zealand. The fact that the government gave away ownership of the intellectual property is one mystery. The Chiron funded conference mentioned earlier is a prime example of how one medical professional is building a reputation and career courtesy of a company whose product she is meant to be trialing in an unbiased way.

Potentially dangerous conflicts of interest extend to the MeNZB™ adverse event monitoring system. This system is overseen by hand picked pro-vaccine specialists. In two cases these specialists are colleagues of the meningococcal B researchers. This "independent" monitoring board has developed a method that only considers known adverse events, discounting deaths following meningococcal vaccination as due to "accident" or "other unrelated illness." It should be noted that the Minister has not denied the two deaths reported to have occurred during the trials. They were dismissed as being not relevant to the vaccination trial. This is at odds with good pharmaco-vigilance practice. . . .

Then there are the ethical questions surrounding the Ministry of Health downloading school rolls into its new National Immunisation Register to capture all children's ID information. Was informed consent granted for that?

The questions surrounding the MeNZB™ vaccine continue to mount. Given that government documents reveal that it was a vaccine made in Norway and not Chiron's Italian made MeNZB™ vaccine that was used in the New Zealand trials, and given that a virtually untested vaccine rolled out "without efficacy data" is now in general use, the primary question may be: is the Chiron MeNZB™ vaccine now being used in the current mass vaccination of 1.1 5 million young New Zealanders itself an uncontrolled medical experiment? . . .

Perhaps a recent comment in the *New York Times* goes some way to explaining the ideology behind it all. In a debate before the US Advisory Committee on Immunization Practices[,] an immunization expert, discussing the introduction of a new meningococcal vaccine[,] said, "Frightening parents about the consequences of failing to vaccinate their children will most likely be part of the campaign. For that task, meningococcal meningitis is ideal."

In New Zealand the Ministry of Health has done more than frighten the public. They appear to have participated in a new orchestrated litany of lies and a massive breach of the public trust.

New Zealand's Mass Meningitis Vaccination Campaign Was a Success

New Zealand Ministry of Health

In the following announcement, issued several years after completion of New Zealand's program for vaccinating children against the
local strain of meningitis B, the New Zealand government's Ministry
of Health declares that it helped curb a devastating epidemic. It
states that full information about the vaccine was widely available
to the public during the campaign and that it was always known that
vaccination might not be effective for everyone. The announcement
also answers questions that people have had about the program
and explains that they should still watch for signs of meningitis
because the vaccine may not provide long-lasting protection, and it
does not protect against other strains of the disease.

The MeNZB™ vaccine has helped curb a devastating epidemic.

Ministry of Health Senior Advisor Public
Health Medicine Dr Alison Roberts says New Zealanders
have always been told that the vaccine, though effective,
may not work for everyone who has it.

SOURCE: New Zealand Ministry of Health, "The MeNZB™ Vaccine
Helped Curb an Epidemic," media release, July 22, 2008. © 2008 New
Zealand Ministry of Health. Reproduced by permission.

"We take very seriously the need to ensure the public has access to full information about the MeNZB™ vaccine. During the campaign, this was provided by advertisements, brochures, consent forms, websites and directly from health professionals."

MeNZB™ consent forms and information booklets told parents that the vaccine protection was expected to last for only a few years but that the exact period of protection was unknown.

"This was the best estimate we had at the time. Ongoing studies will tell us how long protection is likely to last. As more information about effectiveness has become available it has been shared with health professionals because GPs [general practitioners] and practice nurses are the people parents turn to for advice and information about immunisation."

The immunisation website will be updated as new information comes to hand.

A big part of the Meningococcal B Immunisation Programme was educating people about the signs and symptoms of meningococcal disease and other serious illness in their children and the need to seek medical help fast when in doubt because disease can move extremely quickly and be difficult to diagnose.

The Ministry stressed in its communications materials that no vaccine provided 100 per cent effectiveness and that the public needed to remain vigilant for signs of the disease.

The MeNZB™ Vaccine Reduced the Toll Taken by Meningitis

With epidemic strain cases now at the lowest level in a decade, it is clear that the Meningococcal B Immunisation Programme has succeeded in helping to reduce the toll this disease has taken on our communities.

"We must not lose sight of the fact that this is a horrific disease. The MeNZB™ vaccine was developed to help

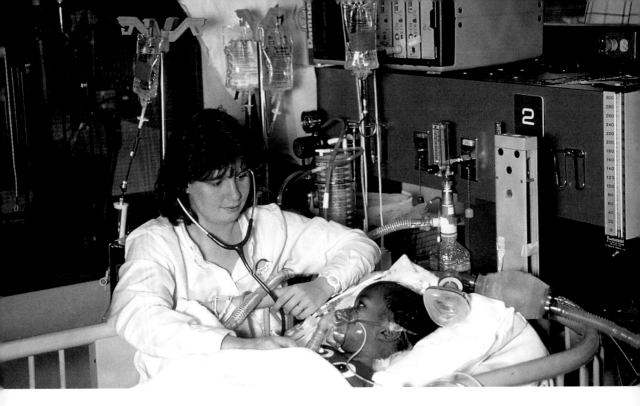

An intensive care unit nurse tends to a child suffering from meningitis. New Zealand officials say that a mass immunization program has reduced the number of cases there. (James Prince/ Photo Researchers, Inc.)

protect against a specific epidemic strain of meningococcal disease and it has acted as a circuit breaker, helping to prevent more cases while the epidemic ran its course."

Although the MeNZB™ vaccine is no longer routinely offered to babies and pre-schoolers, the vaccine is still available if parents believe their child is at special risk and a GP agrees, or where a GP assesses a child or young person under 20 years old is at special risk and should have the vaccine.

Parents of babies who started their MeNZB™ doses before 1 June 2008 are encouraged to complete the course. The vaccine is also available to some high risk groups such as laboratory workers.

What was the purpose of the Meningococcal B Immunisation Programme? The Meningococcal B Immunisation Programme was designed to control an epidemic of a specific strain of meningococcal B disease. The MeNZB™ vaccine was used successfully as a circuit breaker, preventing cases of meningococcal disease during the epidemic. Clinical trials suggest that MeNZB™ protection from meningococcal disease may not be long-term, meaning the vaccine may be best used to stop an epidemic rather than for a long-term schedule vaccine.

What were parents told about MeNZB™ vaccine protection? The MeNZB™ consent form told parents "We expect that most people who receive three doses will be protected against this common strain of meningococcal B disease. Protection is expected to last for a few years but the exact period is unknown. As with all vaccines not everyone fully vaccinated will be protected. The MeNZB™ vaccine will not protect against meningococcal A or C or other strains of B. So you still need to watch out for signs and symptoms of meningococcal disease whether you or your child has been vaccinated or not."

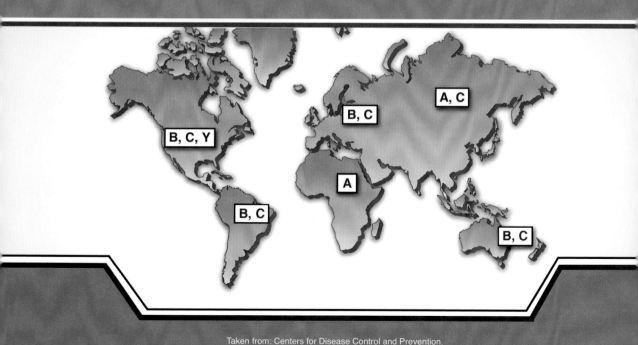

Global Distribution of Different Types of Meningococcal Disease

Taken from: Centers for Disease Control and Prevention.

How much did the Meningococcal B Immunisation Programme cost? The Government committed $200 million to the Meningococcal Vaccine Strategy which paid for the development of a strain-specific vaccine, clinical trials and implementation of our biggest mass immunisation campaign for all New Zealanders under 20 years old. A further $22 million was committed so that if necessary, the programme could continue for children aged under five years until mid 2009.

How many New Zealanders were immunised with MeNZB™? More than one million New Zealanders under the age of 20 years have received one or more doses of MeNZB™ vaccine. In total, 3.4 million doses of vaccine have been given.

What if the epidemic returns in the next few years? The Ministry of Health will continue to monitor meningococcal B disease and will have a supply of MeNZB™ available if disease rates increase substantially.

What do parents need to do now about meningococcal disease? Even though meningococcal B epidemic strain disease rates are low, the disease is still present. The MeNZB™ vaccine protects against the strain of meningococcal B causing the epidemic, but it will not protect against other strains and may not provide long-lasting protection. This is why New Zealanders still need to watch out for the signs and symptoms of this disease, and seek medical help immediately if they are concerned.

What is meningococcal disease? Meningococcal disease is a bacterial infection. It causes severe illnesses including meningitis (an infection of membranes that cover the brain) and septicaemia (a serious infection in the blood). There are several strains of bacteria which cause meningococcal disease including A, B and C. MeNZB™ vaccine was developed to protect against the strain of meningococcal B causing the New Zealand epidemic.

FAST FACT

Meningococcal B rates are five times higher in New Zealand children who have not been immunized than in those who have received MeNZB™, according to an announcement made by the vaccine's manufacturer.

CHAPTER 3

Personal Narratives About Meningitis

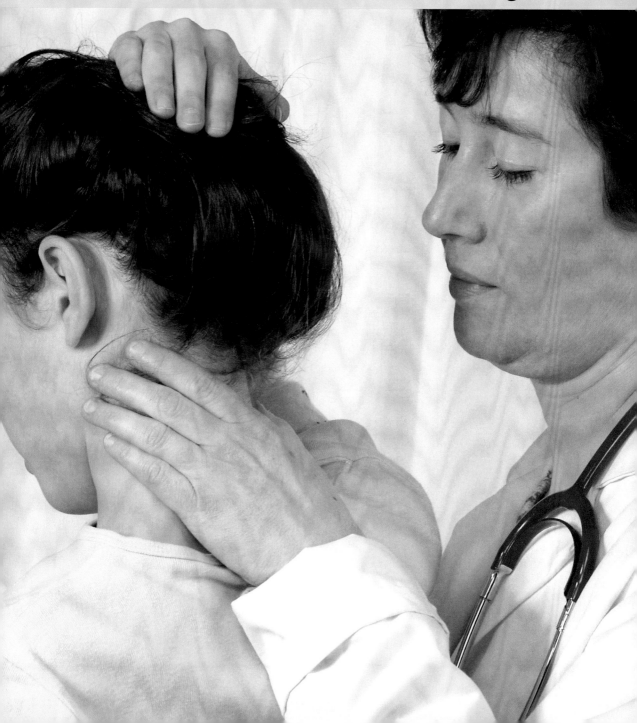

Losing a Daughter to Meningitis

Diane Werner

In the following article Diane Werner writes about the sudden death of her twenty-year-old daughter, Becky, from meningitis. When Becky got sick during the night, her mother thought she had the flu, but it kept getting worse, so she took her to the emergency room. At first the doctor said she just had an ear infection, but soon she was transferred to the intensive care unit (ICU), and that evening she died. Becky Werner's parents have founded the Becky Werner Meningitis Foundation, a nonprofit organization that aims to increase awareness of the dangers of meningitis and the methods of prevention.

O ur story is not unlike the other stories. Our daughter Becky was a beautiful, outgoing, and vivacious 20 year old. She attended our local tech college where she would have graduated in June with a marketing degree and planned on going on to get a degree in graphic arts.

Photo on previous page. A doctor tests a patient's neck, one procedure used to diagnose meningitis. (BSIP/Photo Researchers, Inc.)

SOURCE: Diane Werner, "Becky's Story," The Becky Werner Meningitis Foundation, December 2, 2008. Reproduced by permission.

She had played volleyball since she was in 5th grade. That was her only sport and she loved every minute of it! Both our girls were very active in club volleyball, which took us all around the country playing volleyball. Volleyball was such a part of her life, that she convinced her dad he should coach a team, and that he did . . . hers! When she got to college, she decided that she would like to be a coach and was able to do that for one year. Because she had minor knee problems, she decided to take off a year to give her knees a much needed break.

She could flash a beautiful smile at any given moment as well as light up a room with her presence. She loved everything about life from her friends and family, to the sport of volleyball, animals but especially her precious dog, Rocky, who she trained and teased relentlessly and he loved her to death. One was never without the other.

Sudden Illness

On the morning of Feb 24, 2004, Becky got up complaining she didn't feel well and we suggested that she stay at home, drink plenty of fluids and take ibuprofen. I called her around lunchtime to see if she was okay, she sounded pretty sick but I was sure she had some type of flu. She had been fine the night before and had even gone out to eat with us. When I arrived home from work at 7:00 PM, Becky still did not feel well and said that she had been in bed all day. When she decided to get up for a little while and check her email, she was unsteady and I told [her] to go back to bed and that the email could wait until tomorrow. She went back to bed without any argument.

At 1:00 AM, I found her lying in the hallway, moaning, and I asked her what was wrong. She said that she didn't feel good. When I asked where she was going, she said that she was trying to go to the bathroom. I helped her into the bathroom and then put her back to bed and inquired what she had eaten that day and if she had been drinking fluids. At this time she had no fever and very few complaints. After she had answered all my questions to my satisfaction, I went back to bed and told my husband that I should probably take her to the clinic where I worked to have someone look her over. At 3:00 AM, I now found her lying on the floor next to my bed, moaning. Again, the same circumstances presented themselves. She said that she had been vomiting and now had a small amount of diarrhea. There were no outwards signs of any vomiting and again no fever! By 5:00 AM I found her again in the hallway and started in on a barrage of questions, none of which she could really give me a definitive answer. She complained of being very weak and that she couldn't see! Was it because it was dark, because her eyes were closed, because she didn't have her contacts in, because, because, because. I flipped on the hall way light and when I saw that her eyes were rolling around in her head, we knew she was really sick. Sicker than she had [led] us to believe.

When we arrived at the ER [emergency room], we were still convinced that she had some type of flu. The doctor came in and looked at her and said she had an ear infection but her blood pressure was so low. We mentioned to him that her fingertips were blue and she was complaining of her legs falling asleep. Then a flurry of things started to happen and no one was telling us anything. We never left her side and she kept asking us what was happening to her. They told us that she was being transferred to the ICU and would probably stay there for about two weeks. Two weeks for an ear infection? Every time we asked what was going on, all they could tell us was they weren't sure yet. By the time she did get to the ICU, symptoms started to manifest themselves. No one was calling it meningitis yet. By this time, we were in shock as to what was happening. I have

FAST FACT

According to the National Meningitis Association, adolescents and young adults account for nearly 30 percent of all U.S. cases of meningococcal disease, and fatality rates are up to five times higher among fifteen- to twenty-four year-olds compared with other age groups.

worked in the medical field for 24 years and I could not fathom what was happening to us and especially to her!

A Tragic Ending

The ICU doctor, whom I had known for years, began to unfold what was going on. Some very good friends of ours had arrived and told Becky to call on the name of Jesus and she did! They needed to intubate her immediately [to help her breathe]. I explained to her what they were going to do and her last words were, "OK, Momma." The doctor wanted to do it with her awake because, in hind sight, I believe he knew that if he had sedated her she would not be cognizant again. The intubation was too intolerable for her, so he sedated her.

After Becky Werner (pictured) died suddenly from meningitis at the age of twenty, her parents established the Becky Werner Meningitis Foundation to increase awarness of the dangers of the disease and to provide information on prevention. **(Courtesy of the Becky Werner Meningitis Foundation. Reproduced by permission.)**

By 8:00 PM, he approached me with tears in his eyes and I said, "She's going to die, isn't she?" And he responded with a nod of his head. I asked him what was going to happen next. He informed me that the disease would attack her heart and it would just stop.

By 9:00 PM her heart stopped and she slipped peacefully away with about 30 friends and relatives around her.

We are certain Becky is with Jesus, because His name was one of the last words to come from her lips!

God blessed us with 20 years of memories and not a single one will be forgotten. We will see her again when we are reunited once more in heaven.

We miss you honey!

Vaccination Could Have Prevented a Son's Death

Donna Knutter

The following is a letter Donna Knutter wrote to TV talk show host Oprah Winfrey about the death of her seventeen-year-old son, Alex, who died of meningococcal meningitis only fifteen hours after first feeling sick. She hoped that Winfrey would publicize the need for being vaccinated against meningitis on her show. Alex's illness progressed very suddenly during the night, and when he fell to the floor his parents called 911. By the time they got to the hospital he was unconscious. A few days after Alex's death, his mother learned that there is a vaccine that could have prevented his illness, and she now believes vaccination should be required.

O n Friday, February 23 2007 around 7:30 P.M. our 17 year old son Alex came to me complaining of a headache. I gave him some Tylenol and told him to rest for the night. When I got up around 6:30 Saturday morning he stated he had been vomiting all night. He felt somewhat feverish so I figured it was

SOURCE: Donna Knutter, "About Alex," The Knutter Family Web site, September 2008. www.theknutters.com. Reproduced by permission.

the flu. I told him to get something to drink and go lay down. When I went to check on him a little while later he wouldn't really talk to me, he just sat in the recliner and covered his eyes with his hair. When my husband got up, he noticed Alex sitting in the chair and his lips were somewhat blue. He asked what was going on and Alex wouldn't answer him. I said Alex wasn't feeling good and had been vomiting all night. When my husband went to take a shower, Alex moved from the recliner to the floor and just laid there and moaned and said his heart hurt. I wasn't sure what was going on because Alex could be very dramatic when he wanted to. Thinking maybe it was heartburn I told him to get up and get a glass of milk and then go lay downstairs and watch TV. He went into the kitchen and started to pour a glass of milk but instead just turned and headed downstairs. He got down a few steps and then stumbled to the bottom where he again, laid down on the floor. I went and put the milk away and turned to head downstairs and talk to him. When I got to the bottom of the stairs, he was leaning against the wall with a blank glassy stare and had vomited on himself. I screamed for my husband, grabbed the nearest phone and dialed 911.

I had no idea what was going on and I am ashamed to say I thought maybe he had somehow done this to himself by taking something. I can't even tell you what happened on the phone, but I remember yelling "Alex, what did you take!!" I remember trying to relay information to my husband on how to do CPR until help arrived. I remember it taking way too long for the ambulance to get to our house. I remember the police asking lots of questions. I remember letting the dog out because she was going crazy. I remember praying.

FAST FACT

It is estimated by the American College Health Association that 100 to 125 cases of meningococcal disease occur annually on college campuses, and five to fifteen students die as a result.

When Alex was stable enough to be transported we were told we would have to stay behind and answer questions—like that was going to happen. When we arrived at the hospital we were immediately brought into the family room. A hospital chaplain came to sit with us and a nurse came and got my husband to answer some questions. When he came back to the room, he said they were working on Alex but it didn't look good. They had suggested we call our family. How do you call your family—what do you say?? We called our oldest son who lived in Madison and told him he needed to come home right away. I went to see Alex and was not prepared for what I saw in that room. Of course, how could I be? Alex was unconscious with tubes and monitors everywhere. His skin was purple and he had this terrible rash everywhere I looked. I just went and caressed his hair and whispered to him that he needed to fight this! That I needed him here with me, that grandma needed him, we all needed and loved him. I sat in the room for a minute or two and then could not take it and went to be with my husband. As we sat there waiting the doctor came in to give us an update. They wanted to transfer him to Children's Hospital in Milwaukee, but they couldn't stabilize him. Her exact words—"I don't think your son is going to make it" and that was that—they came and got her and off she went. We sat with the chaplain just stunned beyond comprehension. A few minutes later they came in and said his blood pressure was stabilized and they may be able to transfer him after all. At some point, my mother-in-law showed up and went to see Alex with my husband. After a few minutes, my husband came and got me and said I needed to come to the room because Alex's blood pressure dropped again. Our 17 year old son Alexander John Knutter passed away at 10:36 A.M. on Saturday, February 24 2007 from Meningococcal Meningitis.

Meningitis Vaccination Should Be Required

On Monday, February 26 I learned that there was a vaccine that could have prevented the worst experience of my life. I talked with the Kenosha County Health Department and questioned why—given the swiftness and severity of this disease (it took our son in less than 15 hours) is it not a required immunization? We were even told that had we brought our son to the hospital earlier, because of the symptoms he displayed, he would have been diagnosed with the flu and sent home with directions to rest and get plenty of fluids.

Because of the contagious nature of Meningitis, we were inundated with media attention. They wanted to inform parents of what to look for without causing widespread panic. In one of the articles there was a quote

Students in Ohio await mandatory vaccination. The author, who lost her seventeen-year-old son to meningitis, is a strong believer in mandatory vaccinations for the disease. (Mike Simons/Getty Images)

from a physician stating there were more important things parents should be concerned with like unprotected sex, drugs and drinking. While these are important to discuss with your child, ultimately it is your child's choice that will protect them from these types of things. Our son had no choice when it came to Meningitis. Until that day, we felt like we did everything we could to protect our children. They received all required immunizations. We discussed the dangers of drugs, alcohol, sex, and driving irresponsibly. Had we been aware of this deadly disease—we would have protected them against it as well. We are now learning all we can about all forms of Meningitis and what we can do to prevent another family from having to go through what we went through. We will never experience the joys of graduation, marriage or grandchildren with our son Alex and we will always struggle to understand this loss.

I write to you because I think this is a growing, preventable disease that needs to be addressed. We need to get our story out along with the stories of others who have lost or have survived and the daily struggles they endure. There are many people and organizations that fight everyday to educate all on this deadly and debilitating disease. They do not get the attention they deserve.

A Long Ordeal with Meningitis

Elizabeth Simpson

In the following article Elizabeth Simpson describes what happened to teenager Gerald Pe when he got bacterial meningitis. He felt sick while he was at the beach and thought he had the flu, but by the next morning he was too weak and confused to call anyone. When his mother could not reach him, she called 911. Simpson explains that Pe spent fifty-four days in the hospital and nearly died; he was put on a respirator and the front part of both his feet had to be amputated. Eventually, after eight surgeries to repair his legs, Pe recovered and learned to walk with leg braces, and he was able to finish high school. Simpson is a staff writer for the *Norfolk (VA) Virginian-Pilot* in the Hampton Roads region of Virginia.

W hen Gerald Pe heads to Virginia Tech later this month [August 2008], he'll be required to have a meningitis vaccine or sign a waiver saying he knows the risk of not getting one.

SOURCE: Elizabeth Simpson, "Beach Meningitis Survivor Encourages Others to Get Vaccine," *Norfolk (VA) Virginian-Pilot*, August 11, 2008. Copyright © 2008 The Virginian-Pilot News. Reproduced by permission.

The 20-year-old Virginia Beach man knows the danger all too well.

He narrowly survived a bout with bacterial meningitis—an infection of the fluid around the spinal cord and brain—last year when he was living at home and attending Tidewater Community College.

His parents, Grace and Flodoir Pe, watched in horror on May 1, 2007, as his arms and legs turned from red to dark purple to black in a matter of hours. Infection was racing through his body. His first symptoms—fatigue and backache—had started only 24 hours earlier.

The next six months proved harrowing:

Fifty-four days in Sentara Virginia Beach General Hospital. The front part of both his feet amputated, taking him from a size 12 shoe to a 7. Months of painful removal of dead tissue, skin grafting and physical therapy.

He shares his experience to encourage others to get a vaccine before heading off to college. Virginia is one of 21 states in which students of four-year colleges—a high-risk population—are required to either have the vaccine or sign a waiver. Because he was a community college student last year, he didn't get one.

"Nothing triggered us to get the vaccine," said his mother, Grace Pe, a U.S. Coast Guard security specialist.

Getting Sick

On April 30 of last year, Pe went to the beach with a friend. His back started aching, and the sunlight hurt his eyes. Soon he was having to stop to rest on benches.

He started to feel feverish and figured he was getting the flu, so he went home. He told his mother he had a fever and was going to sleep it off.

He usually wakes up by 8, but the next day he didn't awake until 11 A.M. He stood up but felt so weak he fell back on his bed. He stood up again and made it to his computer chair, which has wheels. He rolled himself to the kitchen to get something to eat and drink.

Then he rolled his chair to the bathroom and took a shower. He sat back down on his chair to roll back to his bedroom. But when he got there, he didn't have the strength to lift the chair over the molding between the hallway and his room.

So he sat there, too weak and confused to call 911 or his parents.

He usually takes his sister, now 13, to the bus stop, but she had called her mother that morning to tell her she had walked because Gerald hadn't gotten out of bed in time. After calling home repeatedly, Grace became concerned and asked her husband [Flodoir] to go home during lunch to check on him.

When Flodoir got there, Gerald was still sitting in the computer chair, barely conscious. He had red splotches up and down his legs and arms. His nose was red and he was hot to the touch.

Flodoir called 911.

PERSPECTIVES ON DISEASES AND DISORDERS

Gerald remembers only snapshots during the next few minutes: being carried on a stretcher down the front stairs of their home. Someone asking him to touch his chin to neck and move his head side to side. Being asked to recite his Social Security number . . . telling them the first three numbers. . . .

And that's all he remembers clearly until he woke up several days later in the intensive care unit.

A Strange Dream

Sometime between those two points, though, he remembers a dream that felt like a near-death experience.

He thought he was on an airplane with a family friend, his cousin and a stranger.

The pilot said he was about to take off, and Gerald insisted on sitting next to the stranger. The family friend put a rosary—with unusually shaped square beads—on his chest.

As the airplane was flying, he saw bright light coming through the front windshield of the airplane.

In the emergency room, meanwhile, his father noticed he looked like he was either crying or laughing, but it was hard to tell because of his oxygen mask.

"Gerald, what's wrong?" Flodoir asked.

"Dad, it's better up here," he said.

Flodoir used to be a Navy corpsmen and had been in a lot of emergency medical situations, but seeing his son's skin turn black in a matter of hours and watching him gasp for air made him feel faint.

About that time, Grace arrived in the emergency room. When she saw her husband, he was so white, she thought he was sick, too.

Grace leaned over her son, and Gerald repeated, "It's actually better up here."

She hit him in the chest and said, "Gerald you can't leave me this way."

He was whisked from the emergency room to the intensive care unit, where he was put on a respirator and a dialysis machine because his kidneys were failing.

Blood tests and a spinal tap showed he had bacterial meningitis and septicemia, a blood infection.

The list of possible outcomes was sobering: brain damage, blindness, kidney failure, amputations, death.

In his dream, he felt as though the plane were landing when he regained consciousness three days later.

Painful Treatments

He gradually improved over his nine days in ICU, where he received IV antibiotics. Once the danger of dying passed, he was moved to another unit of the hospital for treatment of the damaged tissue and skin.

Because meningitis is a communicable disease spread by close contact with bodily fluids, Virginia Beach Health Department officials became involved in the case, advising those closest to him to take a course of antibiotics.

The family never was able, though, to determine just how Gerald contracted the disease.

Once he moved to Room 478, Gerald endured weeks of "debridement," removal of the damaged and dead tissue on his legs.

Tending the wounds took hours, several times a week.

"It felt like they were ripping my skin off."

The first of nine surgeries came on Memorial Day weekend. Gerald expected more debridement to be done, but doctors discovered the tissue was so infected, amputation was needed to prevent more infection.

While Gerald lay unconscious, doctors presented his parents with two options. Amputation of the toes and front part of the foot. Or amputation below the knees, which would give him more mobility because he'd be fitted with prostheses.

FAST FACT

Meningococcal bacteria produce toxins that damage blood vessels. When blood vessels become blocked, the surrounding tissues die, causing gangrene, which can require amputation of limbs.

The parents decided to go the less radical route, figuring Gerald could decide on his own later if he wanted amputation below the knee.

The memory of that decision still haunts Grace. "I hated that consultation room."

Grace and Flodoir thought they would tell Gerald the next morning about what had happened during the surgery, but one of his doctors, who did his rounds early, reached him first and told Gerald about the amputation.

"I cried my eyes out. I bawled," Gerald remembers.

Recovering from Amputation

Eight more surgeries would follow, during which pins were placed in his foot, and skin grafts from one part of his body were used to repair his feet and legs.

He went home in June and over the next few months went from wheelchair to walker to crutches. By December, he could walk using special leg braces.

"I can shoot baskets, but I can't play basketball. I can't run, but I never really liked running anyway. I don't walk as fast, but I can do most everything I used to do."

In February [2008], he returned to the high school he graduated from in 2006, Ocean Lakes, to tell students about his experience, and encourage them to get the vaccine that protects against meningitis.

Later this month, he'll head to Virginia Tech to major in finance.

He never did figure out who the stranger was sitting next to him on the plane in his dream, but the friend who gave him the rosary came to visit the family when he returned home from the hospital that summer.

She prayed a rosary for him and placed it on his chest.

The unusual, square-beaded rosary was the one he remembered from his dream.

Overcoming Amputations to Graduate from College

Jodi Heckel

In the following article Jodi Heckel describes Erica Van Zuidam's recovery from bacterial meningitis. While a freshman at the University of Illinois, Van Zuidam got sick and was taken to the emergency room. Her hands and feet had to be amputated, and she required months of rehabilitation, learning to use her prosthetic arms and legs. But a little more than a year later, she was able to go back to college and eventually to graduate. Now she is starting graduate training in order to become an occupational therapist, to work with patients who need prosthetics. Heckel is a reporter for the Champaign, Illinois, *News-Gazette*.

Erica Van Zuidam was to take her seat in the Assembly Hall this weekend [in May 2009], one graduate in a sea of blue caps and gowns. When her name was called, she would cross the stage and receive her diploma. Just like everyone else.

SOURCE: Jodi Heckel, "After Long Road Back, UI Graduate Moving On," News-Gazette.com, May 17, 2009. © Copyright 2009 The News-Gazette, Inc. All rights reserved. Reproduced by permission.

That's how she wants it. She doesn't want to be noticed because of her prosthetic arms and legs. She doesn't want pity for the consequences of the disease that nearly killed her. She doesn't want any special treatment.

She wants to graduate and go on with her life, with plans for a career helping people much like herself.

To Janice Van Zuidam, Erica's mother, it seems like a million years ago that Erica was getting ready to come back to school. The strategy was to take it one day at a time and see if she could handle it.

"Here we are on the other side of it already," Van Zuidam says.

Erica returned to the University of Illinois [UI] in fall 2006. Her parents worried about how she'd manage getting around the large campus with her prosthetic legs, particularly in bad weather, or living on her own.

Fifteen months earlier, Erica was finishing her freshman year at the UI when she began feeling sick during finals week. She ended up in the emergency room, diagnosed with bacterial meningitis.

She spent several months in the hospital, and her hands and feet had to be amputated because of damage from the disease. Then she began months of rehabilitation to learn to use her new prosthetic arms and legs.

Now she's graduating. In June, she'll begin a graduate program in occupational therapy at Rush University in Chicago. She hopes to work with patients needing prosthetics.

"I'm just amazed that she did it," Van Zuidam says of her daughter. "She gets up every day and faces the day and goes through it—and does what she needs to do."

Erica downplays any obstacles.

"People have been so understanding, willing to help," she says. "I know that they're there if I need them."

Like the time she got stuck in a snowbank.

"I totally wiped out. Just lost my balance, big time," Erica says.

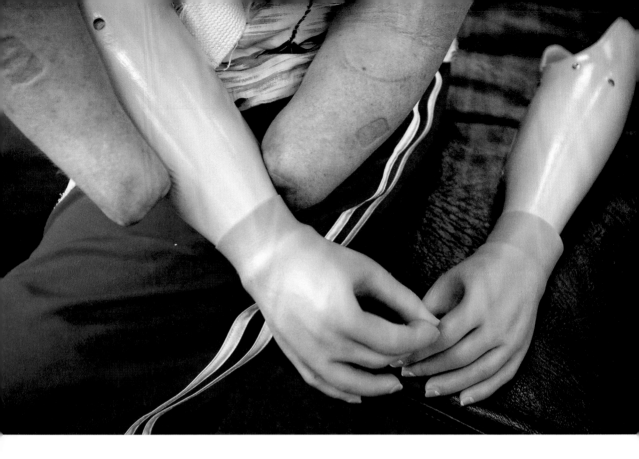

Erica Van Zuidam lost her limbs as the result of a serious bout of bacterial meningitis. She had to learn to use prosthetic arms and legs, such as those shown here. (AP Images)

She asked a stranger to help her out of the snow and to her building for class.

Or like Mary Carlton, who teaches in the kinesiology department. Erica calls her "my Champaign [Illinois] mom.

"She's made my life a lot easier here," Erica says. "She makes certain everything with me is OK, and nothing is a struggle."

Erica has never asked for any special treatment, though, Carlton says: "I don't pamper her. She would hate it if I did that."

She finished college in four years, not counting the time she was at home recovering from her illness, her father points out.

"I'm proud of all three (of my) kids, but especially what she had to overcome to do this," Tim Van Zuidam says.

An Inspiration

Erica is at Westview Elementary School on a late winter afternoon for an after-school jump rope program run by kinesiology students. A few of the younger children wander up to Erica, touching the hooks on the ends of her prosthetic arms.

When the Champaign school program began, Erica told the children how she got sick, lost her hands and feet, and learned how to use her new arms and legs, Carlton says.

"One guy said, 'You're really cool,' and that was the final word, and we moved on," she says.

Erica projects self-confidence, comfortable with who she is, prosthetics and all. She doesn't mind answering questions about what happened to her, especially from kids. But she doesn't want people to make a big deal out of it.

Inevitably, if she's at a gas station or a store, someone will tell her she's amazing, or an inspiration, Erica says, exasperated. She hates standing out.

"I hate it. I hate it a lot," she says. "People focus more on my outward stuff first. If I was who I was four years ago, you wouldn't notice me if I walked in a room. Now you do."

"Erica knows in her heart that she survived for some reason," Carlton says. "Who she becomes is going to be scrutinized all along the way. No matter how irritating in some ways it is to stand out, she's got to accept it and turn around and make it a positive."

Erica doesn't mind the attention if it's used to make young people aware of meningitis and its consequences, and to let them know there is a vaccine.

"We're worried after I leave (the UI), everybody is going to forget about it," Erica says. "It's old news, until it happens again. That makes me sad."

A Good Relationship

Erica met her boyfriend, Luke Tambrini, on a camping trip on Memorial Day weekend three years ago. She says he's goofy. The life of the party, just like her dad.

"We're ripping on each other all the time. My dad teases me constantly, and so does Luke," she says.

Tambrini liked Erica's personality—funny, outgoing, fun-loving.

"And she's cute," he says.

"She wasn't afraid of certain challenges. I think we went tubing that weekend. I thought, if I had no arms and legs, the last place I'd want to be is on the water, flying around behind a boat. She was having a blast."

Tambrini didn't make a big deal out of her disability or make it seem like it was something he had to adjust to, Erica says.

After three years of being together, he knows when to grab her arm if the ground is hilly or she's walking up stairs. He knows how to hand her something so it's easy for her to grasp.

"He just knows the routine," Erica says. "He helps me a lot, but not too much. He knows the little things to do. But I also had to tell him to back off a little bit."

Erica and Luke like to hang out with friends, and they have their favorite Mexican restaurant in his hometown of Dyer, [Indiana].

They tried Rollerblading once, in the basement of Erica's parents' house. It didn't work out.

Tambrini doesn't mind the things they can't do because of Erica's disability.

"Relationships are about sacrifice," he says. "There are certain things you do for the people you love."

Erica says the two definitely have a future together, after she finishes graduate school.

Career Plans

When Erica returned to the UI, she transferred to the kinesiology department, with plans to pursue occupational therapy as a career. She hopes to offer patients the perspective of someone who uses prosthetics.

Last summer, she volunteered with Kristi Turner, her occupational therapist at the Rehabilitation Institute of Chicago.

One of Turner's patients at the time was a woman who was a quad amputee, like Erica. She was having a tough time psychologically, dealing with what had happened to her, Turner says.

Seeing Erica made all the difference.

"She just loved talking to Erica. It was very big inspiration to her," Turner says. "She is seeing this beautiful young girl that is in the exact same situation she is in and is doing wonderfully."

Erica helped the woman find the best way to hold a toothbrush, or to do her hair or put on makeup.

"We had a lot of fun," she says. "It was good to know that I'm going to like what I'm going to be doing."

Tim Van Zuidam recently recalled a day shortly after Erica got sick.

She was in intensive care, and her doctor told the Van Zuidams that Erica would lose both her hands, her right foot and part of her left foot. Would she be able to live like that?

If not, the medical staff could stop trying to save her life and just make her comfortable, he said. It was an option he had to present.

No way, Tim Van Zuidam said.

"Wow, what if somebody would have made that decision?" he thinks now. "Now she's going to graduate, go on to graduate school, become an occupational therapist, and who knows how many people she'll influence."

For Turner, seeing Erica now "is probably the most rewarding thing to me, because we don't always see the end result.

"To see she accomplished everything we hoped she would, and that we knew she could."

> ## FAST FACT
>
> According to the American College Health Association, since the initiation of routine vaccination of recruits, there has been an 87 percent reduction in sporadic cases and a virtual elimination of outbreaks of invasive meningococcal disease in the U.S. military.

Something to Contribute

Urbana [Illinois] is bittersweet for Erica and her family.

"Even though I love this place so much, it still has this vibe," Erica says, remembering the places she was when she got sick.

"But so many good things have come from it."

She is still the outgoing person she was before she got sick.

Her father says he and his daughter still drive each other nuts sometimes, and she and her siblings pick on each other, just like before.

"She still buys just as many shoes as she did before," he says.

Her faith is stronger now, too.

"I have more of a sense that my life has a very specific path," Erica says. "I think I have something to contribute."

GLOSSARY

antibody	A protein produced by the body's reaction to an antigen; an antibody acts against an antigen through an immune response.
antigen	A substance that causes the production of an antibody upon entering the body.
aseptic meningitis	Another name for viral meningitis.
bacterial meningitis	A form of meningitis caused by bacteria.
conjugate vaccine	A vaccine in which a polysaccharide is linked to a protein that makes it more immunogenic, that is, more able to produce immunity. Newer vaccines against bacterial meningitis are conjugate vaccines.
***Haemophilus influenzae* type B**	The scientific name of the bacterium that can cause HiB meningitis.
herd immunity	An immunity to a disease among unvaccinated people because of the immunity among the vaccinated individuals within the population.
HiB meningitis	The form of meningitis caused by the bacterium *Haemophilus influenzae* type B, against which infants are routinely vaccinated.
immunization	The administration of components of living or dead viruses or bacteria to mount an immune reaction (e.g., antibodies) to the infection, also called vaccination or inoculation.
incubation	The period of time from when a virus or bacterium enters the body until symptoms begin.
gangrene	The death of soft tissues due to loss of blood supply. It can be caused by septicemia.

lumbar puncture	A medical procedure, often called a spinal tap, in which a thin needle is inserted into the spine to obtain fluid to be tested for the presence of bacteria that cause meningitis.
MCV4	The generic name for the vaccine marketed as Menactra. It is a conjugate vaccine.
Menactra	One of the newest vaccines against meningococcal disease, now recommended for everyone between the ages of eleven and eighteen.
meninges	The thin linings that surround the brain and the spinal cord.
meningitis	An inflammation of the fluid and membranes (meninges) surrounding the spinal cord and the brain.
meningococcal disease	The form of meningitis produced by the bacterium *Neisseria meningitidis.*
Neisseria meningitidis	The scientific name of the bacterium that can cause meningococcal disease.
outbreak	A minimum of three cases of a disease from the same community or institution within three months' time.
pneumococcal meningitis	The form of meningitis caused by the bacterium *Streptococcus pneumoniae.*
polysaccharide	A coating of sugar molecules that are unique antigens in some harmful bacteria.
polysaccharide vaccine	A vaccine made from the components of a long chain of polysaccharides that come from the outer coat of a bacterium. Older vaccines against bacterial meningitis are polysaccharide vaccines.
Prevnar	One of the newest vaccines against pneumococcal meningitis, now standard for infants and toddlers.
septicemia	An infection of the blood, sometimes called "blood poisoning."

serology	The science that deals with the properties and reactions of serums, especially blood serum.
serotype or serogroup	A group of closely related bacteria that have similar antigens.
serum	The watery portion of an animal fluid remaining after coagulation. Blood serum is the liquid component of blood that remains after blood has coagulated, or clotted.
spinal meningitis	Another name for meningococcal disease, commonly used in the past.
Streptococcus pneumoniae	The scientific name of the bacterium that can cause pneumococcal meningitis.
vaccine	A biologic product that produces immunity to a certain infectious disease.
viral meningitis	A form of meningitis caused by a virus.

CHRONOLOGY

1805   Meningococcal disease is first described in medical literature during an outbreak in Geneva, Switzerland.

1806   The first documented case of meningitis in the United States occurs in Medford, Massachusetts.

1840   An epidemic of meningitis in Africa is reported for the first time.

1887   *Neisseria meningitidis*, the bacterium that causes meningococcal disease, is identified.

1910   Throughout the first decade of the twentieth century, the mortality rate for meningococcal disease is 75 to 80 percent.

1913   A treatment for meningitis with antiserum produced in horses results in a marked decrease in mortality from meningococcal disease.

1918   During Word War I meningococcal disease kills 39 percent of the U.S. soldiers who come down with it and sometimes creates panic in army camps.

1928   A meningitis epidemic in the United States with a high mortality rate causes doctors to lose faith in the serums then used to treat it.

1935   Improved serums and antitoxins for treating meningitis are developed.

1937   Sulpha drugs are recognized as effective against meningitis and, over the next few years, they greatly reduce the fatality rate.

1942   *Time* magazine reports that meningococcal disease is on the rise again and that, in army camps, the hysteria caused by the disease appears to be nearly as difficult to cope with as the disease itself.

1944   Penicillin is reported to be effective against meningitis.

1978   The first meningococcal vaccines, which protect against only two of the five types of the disease, are introduced.

1981   Menomune, a polysaccharide vaccine that becomes the standard form of protection against meningococcal disease, is approved by the U.S. Food and Drug Administration (FDA).

1982   The U.S. Army vaccinates all recruits against meningococcal disease.

1985   The first vaccine that protects against HiB meningitis is introduced.

1987   The first conjugate vaccine against HiB is approved by the FDA and is considered significantly more effective than the previous vaccines.

1993   The first vaccine against HiB for infants is introduced, with the potential of wiping out that form of the disease.

1996   The largest epidemic of meningitis in history occurs in Africa.

1997   The American College Health Association recommends that colleges and universities inform all students and their parents about the risk of meningococcal disease and that the schools ensure that all students have access to the vaccine.

2000   Prevnar, a vaccine against pneumococcal meningitis, is approved by the FDA.

2004 New Zealand begins a two-year campaign to vaccinate all children with a controversial new vaccine against meningococcal disease type B, for which no vaccine exists elsewhere.

2005 Menactra, an improved vaccine against meningococcal disease, is approved by the FDA for people aged eleven to fifty-five. The Centers for Disease Control and Prevention recommends that it be given to all eleven- to twelve-year-olds, students entering high school, and college freshmen living in dorms.

2007 Approval of Menactra is extended to include children aged two to ten.

2008 Health authorities in countries of the African meningitis belt commit themselves to introducing the new conjugate vaccine MenAfriVac, designed to prevent periodic epidemics of the disease.

2009 A major epidemic of meningitis in Africa is brought under control through widespread vaccination; the first U.S. vaccine against meningococcal disease type B completes clinical trials and is scheduled to be submitted to the FDA for approval in 2010.

ORGANIZATIONS TO CONTACT

The editors have compiled the following list of organizations concerned with the issues debated in this book. The descriptions are derived from materials provided by the organizations. All have publications or information available for interested readers. The list was compiled on the date of publication of the present volume; the information provided here may change. Be aware that many organizations take several weeks or longer to respond to inquiries, so allow as much time as possible.

American College Health Association (ACHA)
891 Elkridge Landing Rd., Ste. 100,
Linthicum, MD 21090
(410) 859-1500
fax: (410) 859-1510
www.acha.org

The ACHA is a leadership organization for the field of college health and provides services, communications, and advocacy that help its members to advance the health of their campus communities. The "Meningitis on Campus" section of its Web site contains a slide show with extensive material about the disease, including charts and graphs.

Centers for Disease Control and Prevention (CDC)
1600 Clifton Rd.,
Atlanta, GA 30333
(800) 232-4636
www.cdc.gov/menin gitis/index.html

The CDC is a major component of the U.S. Department of Health and Human Services. Its mission is to create the expertise, information, and tools that people and communities need to protect their health. Its Web pages for meningitis have detailed information about the disease and about vaccination against it, including a video and a podcast.

Confederation of Meningitis Organisations (COMO)
www.comoonline.org

The mission of COMO is to assist member organizations to be sustainable, identifiable, and influential sources for information and support services for those people affected by meningitis in their regions. COMO is committed to the elimination of meningitis and septicemia. Its Web site contains a section titled "Faces of Meningitis" that includes the personal stories of meningitis victims.

Doctors Without Borders
333 Seventh Ave., 2nd Fl., New York, NY 10001-5004
(212) 679-6800
fax: (212) 679-7016
http://doctorswithout borders.org

Doctors Without Borders/Médecins Sans Frontières (MSF) is an international medical humanitarian organization that provides aid in nearly sixty countries to people whose survival is threatened by violence, neglect, or catastrophe. Its Web site contains information about the epidemic of meningitis in Africa and its program for mass vaccination in various African countries.

Fight Meningitis
Sanofi Pasteur Inc.
Discovery Dr.
Swiftwater, PA 18370
www.fightmeningitis
.com

This site is provided as a public service by the pharmaceutical company Sanofi Pasteur. In addition to basic information about meningitis, it contains a flash presentation describing in detail how meningitis affects the body at different stages of the disease.

MedlinePlus: Meningitis
www.nlm.nih.gov/med lineplus/meningitis
.html

MedlinePlus is a service of the U.S. National Library of Medicine and the National Institutes of Health. Its meningitis section has a tutorial that can be watched either interactively or as a self-playing presentation or downloaded in PDF form.

Meningitis Angels
www.meningitis-
angels.org

Meningitis Angels is a nonprofit, publicly supported organization that educates the public, schools, day care providers, colleges, government, and media about bacterial meningitis and its prevention, including immunizations. It also offers support groups and message boards for survivors of meningitis and their families. Its Web site offers news and resource information, plus the detailed stories of survivors and of people who died from the disease.

**Meningitis
Foundation of
America (MFA)**
PO Box 1818,
El Mirage, AZ 85335
(480) 270-2652
www.meningitisfoun
dationofamerica.org

The MFA is a nonprofit organization that works to help support sufferers of meningitis and their families, to educate the public and medical professionals about meningitis so that its early diagnosis and treatment will save lives, and to support the development of vaccines. Its Web site offers information, news, survivor stories, and a forum.

**Meningitis Research
Foundation (MRF)**
Midland Way
Thornbury, Bristol
BS25 2BS, UK
www.meningitis.org

The MRF is a nonprofit British organization with over fifteen thousand individual members and supporters. The foundation is working toward a world free from meningitis and septicemia. Its Web site contains information about the disease and recent research, as well as pictures and stories of survivors.

**Meningitis Research
Foundation of Canada**
PO Box 28015, R.P.O.
Parkdale, Waterloo
ON N2L 6J8, Canada
www.meningitis.ca

The Meningitis Research Foundation of Canada is dedicated to the prevention of meningitis, improving survival rates and outcomes, and supporting families of those whose lives have been changed by this disease. It focuses on education and the funding of research. Its Web site contains many survivor stories, as well as information about the disease.

Meningitis Vaccine Project (MVP)
World Health Organization, PATH-Europe
13 chemin du Levant, Bâtiment Avant-Centre, 01210 Ferney-Voltaire, France
www.meningvax.org

The MVP's mission is to eliminate meningitis as a public health problem in sub-Saharan Africa through the development, testing, introduction, and widespread use of conjugate meningococcal vaccines. Its Web site contains archived newsletters and news releases, plus detailed answers to frequently asked questions about the project.

National Meningitis Association (NMA)
738 Robinson Farms Dr., Marietta, GA 30068
(866) 366-3662
fax: (877) 703-6096
www.nmaus.org

The NMA's mission is to educate families, medical professionals, and others about bacterial meningitis and prevention approaches to the disease, focusing in particular on raising awareness and protection among adolescents and young adults. Its Web site contains information and news about the disease, including videos. It also features programs such as M.O.M.s (Moms on Meningitis), a coalition of mothers from across the country whose children's lives have been drastically affected by meningococcal disease; and T.E.A.M. (Together Educating Against Meningitis), a volunteer program dedicated to educating the public about meningococcal disease.

Voices of Meningitis
National Association of School Nurses
8484 Georgia Ave. Ste. 420, Silver Spring MD 20910
www.voicesofmeningitis.org

Voices of Meningitis is a meningococcal disease prevention campaign from the National Association of School Nurses. Its Web site features video presentations by survivors of the disease and families of those who have died from it.

FOR FURTHER READING

Books

Connie Goldsmith, *Meningitis*. Minneapolis, MN: Twenty-First Century, 2008.

ICON Health Publications, *Bacterial Meningitis—A Medical Dictionary, Bibliography, and Annotated Research Guide to Internet References*. San Diego, CA: ICON Health, 2004.

Lorrie Klosterman, *Meningitis*. New York: Benchmark, 2006.

Mark Patinkin, *Up and Running: The Inspiring True Story of a Boy's Struggle to Survive and Triumph*. New York: Center Street, 2005.

Brian Shmaefsky, *Meningitis*. Philadelphia, PA: Chelsea House, 2010.

Periodicals

Karen Fanning, "Meningitis Scare," *Scholastic Choices*, February/March 2008.

Denise Grady, "5 Develop Nerve Disorder After Receiving Meningitis Vaccine," *New York Times*, October 1, 2005.

Mike LaForgia, as told to Irene S. Levine, "The Iron Man: A Meningitis Miracle," *Reader's Digest*, January 2008.

Carolyn Sayre, "Warning Signs of Meningitis," *New York Times*, February 13, 2009.

———"A Lifesaving Vaccine for College Freshmen," *New York Times*, May 7, 2009.

Beth Shapouri, "I Almost Died in My Dorm Room," *Cosmo Girl*, October 2007.

Kate Traynor, "All Adolescents Need Meningitis Vaccination, Experts Say," *American Journal of Health*, September 15, 2007.

USA Today, "Infant Vaccine Against Meningitis Shows Promise," January 9, 2009.

———"Kids Vaccine Slashes Meningitis," January 15, 2009.

Internet Sources

Allafrica, Africa: New Meningitis Vaccine Nears Debut," March 12, 2009. http://allafrica.com/stories/200903120711.html.

Connie Barr, Karen Aarre, and Kjell Persen, "Norway MENZB Doco: Exported Controversial Vaccine," Scoop, October 7, 2006. www.scoop.co.nz/stories/HL0610/S00257.htm.

Anthony Browne, "Medicine's Tragic Price," Observer, November 4, 2001. www.guardian.co.uk/education/2001/nov/04/medicalscience.health.

Arthur Caplan, "Meningitis Shots Should Be Required," MSNBC, September 6, 2007. www.msnbc.msn.com/id/20630968.

Guardian, "Parents and GPs Warned Not to Mistake Meningitis for Swine Flu," September 1, 2009. www.guardian.co.uk/society/2009/sep/01/swine-flu-meningitis-symptoms.

Jenny Hope, "Meningitis B Vaccine Could Be Only Three Years Away," Mail on Sunday, May 15, 2008. www.mailonsunday.co.uk/health/article-566476/Meningitis-B-vaccine-years-away.html.

Nick Horley, "Sting in the Tail for Meningitis Survivors," Telegraph, March 26, 2007. www.telegraph.co.uk/health/children_shealth/3347979/Sting-in-the-tail-for-meningitis-survivors.html.

Andi Hui, "Meningitis Nightmare," Humber Et Cetera, November 20, 2008. www.humberetc.com/displayArticle.php?id=1203&sid=41.

Susan Donaldson James, "For Parents, College Meningitis Deaths Still Evoke Pain," ABC News, September 6, 2007. http://abcnews.go.com/Health/story?id=3562888.

Kindra Kerp, "When the Word 'Meningitis' Darkens the Room," Portland Community College Library, March 1, 2008. www.pcc.edu/library/news/prize/meningitis.pdf.

Sarah Lovinger, "Vaccines Save Lives: Here's Proof," Huffington Post, June 9, 2009. www.huffingtonpost.com/sarah-lovinger/vaccines-save-lives-heres_b_212702.html.

Mail on Sunday, "Miracle Man: Builder Survives Deadly Meningitis Eleven Times in 16 Years," May 6, 2009. www.dailymail.co.uk/health/article-1177581/Miracle-man-Builder-survives-deadly-meningitis-ELEVEN-times-16-years.html.

Medical News Today, "Survey Looks at Black Parents' Knowledge of Meningitis Risks," October 31, 2008. www.medicalnewstoday.com/articles/127696.php.

National Council of State Legislatures, "50 State Summary of Meningitis Legislation and State Laws," September 2009. www.ncsl.org/default.aspx?tabid=13960.

Zablon Odhiambo, "New Vaccine to Stall African Meningitis Epidemics," Science and Development Network, June 15, 2007. www.scidev.net/en/news/new-vaccine-to-stall-african-meningitis-epidemics.html.

David Riedel, "Perfect Conditions," Fairfield Weekly, January 1, 2009. www.fairfieldweekly.com/article.cfm?aid=11140.

Jayne Robinson, "My Daughter's Battle with Meningitis," Parents First for Health, January 2, 2008. www.childrenfirst.nhs.uk/families/real_life/archive/meningitis_jayne.html.

Katie Strickland, "UC Should Take Shot at Mandating Vaccine," Daily Bruin, October 11, 2007. www.dailybruin.ucla.edu/stories/2007/oct/11/emstricklandem.

UNICEF, "A Shot to Live: Meningitis Immunization in Chad," May 8, 2009. www.unicef.org/infobycountry/chad_49620.html.

University Corporation for Atmospheric Research, "UCAR Weather Forecasts Aim to Reduce African Meningitis Epidemics," November 19, 2008. www.ucar.edu/news/releases/2008/meningitis.jsp.

Judith Woods, "The Menace of Meningitis," Telegraph, September 3, 2007. www.telegraph.co.uk/health/children_shealth/3351048/The-menace-of-meningitis.html.

Web Site

NOVA: Killer Disease on Campus (www.pbs.org/wgbh/nova/meningitis). This television presentation about meningitis was aired by the PBS documentary series NOVA. The Web site for it contains articles, animations, and a transcript of the program. The video is available for purchase.

INDEX